The Protocol

and

Etiquette

For

Successful Couples

Yelina Nieto

Photos

Cover: **https://www.everlastingcinema.com/**

Back cover: **https://alvaroching.com/**

Inside: **https://pixabay.com/es**

https://www.freepik.com/ and family files.

Dinnerware, cutlery and accessories ideas:

https://siscanigroup.com/

https://elpatiodeloscorotos.com/

Editing by Mirsa Quintanilla and Valerie Ellis

https://www.yelinanieto.com/
yelinanieto@yahoo.com
@yelinanieto

ISBN: 978-1-7336489-7-4

Dedication

To all young *millennials* starting with my children - and those not as young - who would like to have ideas on how to start and/or to maintain a rewarding and lasting relationship.

Prologue

When author, Yelina Nieto, told me about her desire to write a book in which the etiquette rules would be applied in relation to the love field, I found the idea very original and interesting. I have not found any other works on this subject, at least in our Spanish language. With this, the book that she gives us is of great value to all those who have a partner or aspire to have one. Within the framework of a relationship guided by good manners & moral principles, the author leads us by the hand spontaneously, colloquially, and intimately on the path of building a loving relationship. From the moment he and she meet each other - going through the first kiss to the point where they both become intimate.

Chapter I outlines, in a practical way, how and where to search for a partner. Chapter II puts us on the exciting terrain of "The 5 Languages of Love" - based on Gary Chapman's book, to assertively define what we really want from a relationship and from our future spouse/partner from self-knowledge and other persons.

Regarding the importance of maintaining those good manners that we showed at the beginning of the romance, I fully agree with the author. I know that many of the couples who come to see me in my office have forgotten the application of the Golden Rule in their own homes. They treat a stranger better - someone they had never seen before – rather than the person chose to accompany them for the rest of their lives. Good treatment must be preserved during conflicts, discussions, and crises. Unfortunately, when we are mad, we forget that the human being in front of us is the most important person in our lives. So, both our verbal and nonverbal language comes down to the ill-treatment we would give our worst enemy. But let us keep in mind that our spouse/partner is not our enemy. He is our ally. We formed a team and made a pact of mutual respect that should not be broken.

Chapter III refers to the beginning of the relationship. The author gives us her opinion on the age difference between the couple. Among other topics to consider is online dating as a valid method to get to know someone. This chapter also suggests that we evaluate well the levels of compatibility with the person we date, especially the values that govern their life.

In Chapter IV we are suggested not to hasten the arrival of the passionate kiss; and I agree with that. Numerous studies have shown that a well-given kiss is the bridge to sexual encounter. Through saliva, man transmits testosterone to the woman and vice versa, and both are ignited with increased sexual desire. If this kiss is shared before we get to know each other, at least slightly well, it can obfuscate reason and lead us to live the experience of a "blind" love." And this is even more so if there is premature sex.

In Chapter V, we are advised not to enter the marriage commitment if one or both of us have the word "divorce" written on the forehead as an escape route when things are not going well. As the author tells us: "This would be like investing in a company – which you consider successful at first – with the idea of it failing."

Chapter VI comes loaded with good advice to make the long-awaited intimate encounter unforgettable, considering details that many people overlook. Finally, in Chapter VII, the author essentially ventures into the emotional and spiritual terrain with the "7 C", based on her book "Living in Harmony," which will help us to have a good relationship; and provides some valuable final recommendations, such as:

▪ Learn to share belongings and space in general, starting with our bed. ▪ Find a way to improve each day for family well-being. ▪ Focus on the positive. ▪ Be tolerant of differences. ▪ Be faithful. ▪ Forgive myself. ▪ Get out of the everyday routine whenever we can.

This is an excellent book of protocol and etiquette for a successful relationship. The author's advice advances the possibilities for coexistence in harmony for those couples who want to build a solid, happy, and lasting relationship.

Cecilia Alegria -Dr. Love.

Introduction

In today's life- where time passes in a flash – we seek precision and want everything in a practical and direct way. From the moment that we wake up, in the blink of an eye, we are back in our beds and ready to sleep. Since we spend a third of our lives sleeping, we would like to have pleasant company with us before we sleep, during our sleep and when we wake up. We also want to have someone to accompany us to the cinema, to the theater, to a good restaurant, travel with us and that, if the relationship already passes to another level, to become our life companion with the corresponding civil or ecclesiastical legality, or both. That is why in this book, I want to transmit experiences, knowledge, and useful information – in a simple, accurate, and direct way that guide you in the search for the person that is compatible with you. And I hope that you find this person! I added anecdotes based on real-life cases that will guide and illustrate my points for you.

Likewise, we know that when we die, we will only take away our experiences and knowledge. In this new millennium, people feel a great need to understand themselves and that is why a large group of authors motivated by these concerns, have written books related to mindfulness. Similarly, other colleagues, better known as coaches, have provided guidance and training in specific subjects. Many authors have devoted attention to Carl Jung's archetypes, family constellations and other similar subjects. These are topics that, without a doubt, help us to get to know each other better day by day.

On the other hand, it is important to know how to live with others under different circumstances that will appear in our lives. For example, to find our Prince Charming or the ideal woman, to get married and live happily ever after. That is why today I present to you my new book, "The Protocol and Etiquette for Successful Couples." I wish it will be of good help so that the experiences you have with your partner will be so pleasant and that your partner will accompany you for the rest of your life.

It happens that when we observe a couple in love who have been together for many years, and in a stable relationship, we sometimes ask ourselves: How did this bond begin? What is their secret? How have they lasted so long and remained happy? And there is the detail! Because what starts well, has a better chance of ending well. In this book I will give you a perspective from the angle oriented toward the way you act with your partner, and based on social principles and norms, protocol, and good manners.

You will notice the frequent use of number seven (7). According to experts in numerology, the number seven (7) is the union of number three (3) which means the supreme, and perfection; and the number four (4) that is related to the orientation of Earth, and the cardinal points. Therefore, the number seven (7) is a number where heaven, and earth meet. Wonderful! If we connect it to the couple.

In another order of ideas, if we relate number seven (7) to our day-to-day life, we will notice it in examples known to all, such as: the seven dwarfs of Snow White, seven days a week, etc. On the other hand, it is a good topic of research, and conversation with your future loved one. And if you are a music lover, you are sure to be an expert in using the seven (7) musical notes. Based on this, and with the Kabbalah that has accompanied us for centuries, I have decided to share with you seven (7) wonderful chapters that will enrich your lives, and help acquire ample knowledge about: The Protocol and Etiquette for Successful Couples.

I wish to share with you that, although the motivation to write this book was this beautiful generation of millennials, my words are for anyone who enjoys having a better relationship with others, and benefits from reading this book.

Kind regards,

Yelina Nieto
Author/Writer

Table of Contents

Chapter *One*

♥ Quest for Love

"The soul that can speak through the eyes, can also kiss with a gaze." Gustavo Adolfo Bécquer.

When we think of love, a beautiful poem or a song comes to mind that we would like to share with the ideal partner. We search for that being to become our friend, confidante, companion of talks, dances and trips, our lover, and perhaps also fulfill other functions such as "the multitasking person." However, to find it – or keep the one we already have – it is advisable to read this book: " The Protocol and Etiquette for Successful Couples."

It is important to consider where you will look for your soul mate, that partner with whom you would like to share your ideas, projects, joys, sorrows, and even that intimate relationship desired by both. Therefore, it is of great importance to know who you are going to dedicate your time, and your energy to; because if you have good material, you can create a good piece of furniture. If we compare it to the land where we want to sow, what would you do? You are not going to plant on rocky or arid ground because you know the results are not going to be the ones you expected. So, if you want to look for the ideal match – it is advisable to know what the right conditions are – to make that dream come true. Often, my mother used to tell me to always relate to people who were well-mannered, and even more so, when it came to a boyfriend.

For example, we could start a new relationship where through the exchange of ideas, and sharing several moments, the relationship could be modified according to the circumstances that are presented to us in the future. And with those acquaintances who do not inspire us confidence – even to strike up a healthy friendship – they will not go from knowing that we were born like everyone else, from a father and a mother; because our intuition warns us that this person is unreliable. Some of our interactions may be with people who do not feel Cupid's arrow at the beginning of the relationship. Perhaps –over time – they could become wonderful friends because, although there is the intellectual condition that binds them, the necessary chemistry for a loving relationship is lacking. And let us remember that without this important ingredient... it would be a forced step towards intimacy. Another alternative would be to fall in love through contact with that person. By the way they act, think, by the attraction that from the beginning existed or begins to flourish; and, thanks to small details. Like, for example, bringing some beautiful flowers to the girl when he visits, or the girl could – in turn – pay attention to the person she is interested in.

Once upon a time, I asked my 20-year-old godson, what should a person who would like to find a partner do first? and he said: "Before we want to meet someone else, we must begin by knowing ourselves." I thought his answer was perfectly accurate. So, I will discuss with you how to look for the ideal partner considering that the younger we are, the more alternatives there are. When I say young, I do not mean teens. I remember one of my children at the age of twelve asked me one day if he could have a girlfriend, and my answer was this: *a girlfriend is a person we want to know better and intend to marry*. Consequently, he at his young age could have a special friend that he liked, because he was understandably too young to think about marriage.

Sometimes parents play their sons' game and even find it funny when they say they have multiple girlfriends. Unfortunately, some of these guys do not give the true meaning to courtship. According to the Merriam Webster dictionary, courtship has been defined as: "The act, process, or period of courting - to engage in social activities leading to engagement and marriage." So, you already must be old enough to take the first step and start dating the person who has the basic characteristics you have already chosen on your priority list.

At the beginning of a relationship, we can only notice the physical appearance of the person. However, with contact with him or her, we will realize whether he or she has an education compatible with ours or not. For example: similar principles, and a good level of affinity. Through their behavior you will realize how they act, and with conversation you will know how his or her mental aspects work.

Sometimes, some girls desperately looking to get a boyfriend, study a career they dislike only waiting for Prince Charming. Some reach their goal; others fail to achieve their college degree and abandon the career – ending without a boyfriend and without a university degree. The recommendation for both sexes would be to study the career they are truly passionate about. And if by circumstances of fate your future spouse is among the other students of the faculty/university, they will leave doubly favored. That is, with a partner and with a college degree. Because today not only men but also women must prepare academically. Always remember that what is convenient... will come.

There is a popular saying, *A fox in the hen house.* This saying used to be told to me by a classmate of the university, making me understand that there is no friendship between a man and a woman. However, there are times when friends could later become boyfriends, and then husbands. Likewise, there are countless cases where friendship continues to exist between a man, and a woman over time. Especially with those friends who have been cultivated since adolescence without necessarily getting involved lovingly.

You, the younger ones who are reading this book, some of you rush into the assumption that mixing a sexual relationship with a friendly relationship will allow the birth of love, and it is not necessarily true. First, love is born in the friendly relationship, and then one thinks about having sex, and exchanging intimate preferences. Otherwise the beautiful friendship that could have continued between the two, would simply be at high risk of being lost due to the mixture of emotions misinterpreted by both.

Anecdote

A university student studying in Spain – she was from Chile, though – fell in love with a guy who was also a foreigner. At the end of their studies, each had to return to their home country. At that time, they understood that they could not continue together, and the wonderful moments they had shared in their university years had come to an end. They had dreamed up to that point that a miracle would happen, but the reality was that their beautiful feelings had no future. They had to end their love affair because she could not live in the place where he belonged, and he had to go back to his home country and assume his position in the family business. With great sadness they continued only with a beautiful friendship.

It is also important to know what stage of your life you are in. If you are studying a career that requires a lot of your time and your energy, it is advisable to focus on one thing at a time. What is convenient will come at the right time, – at the end of the day everything has its moment –, and nothing happens sooner or later than it should. It is recommended not to make any important decisions before fulfilling the first six months of mutual knowledge within a relationship. It is worth noting that, during the period of blind love, we usually see all circumstances through rose colored glasses. At this stage, we see situations more beautiful than they really are, and we do not listen to anyone. Well, watch out there, because not all that glitters is gold. On the other hand, what could happen when you are spending your time on someone who does not deserve you? You are avoiding the opportunity to meet a person more suitable for you – who deserves your energy, your time, and your money. Here is a real-life illustration:

Once upon a time there was a prince who was very shy, and very much in love with a princess, who he always saw sitting on a beautiful bench in the park that he visited daily. Day after day, he tried to overcome his shyness, without achieving it. Until one day, he filled himself with courage and after practicing for hours how he was going to introduce himself to his idolized princess, he arrived at the park and found that the princess was accompanied by a knight. With great sadness he walked away thinking that the beautiful protagonist of his dreams already had an admirer. The princess saw him leave without knowing his true feelings. Unfortunately, he decided to stop frequenting the park and forget about his beloved. The sad thing about the story is that the princess did not have a boyfriend, he was her brother, but the shy prince never risked confessing his love.

Sometimes we think – because of our emotional insecurities – that we must have someone by our side; we believe that it is not good to be alone or we consider that we will fill the void we feel by having around people who bring nothing to our lives and that in addition, would subtract time and energy from us. In fact, we could make the mistake of choosing a wrong partner who could destroy our self-esteem to make us believe that without that person we are worthless. This is a huge mistake. There are persons who decide to be alone of their own free will, that is, because they want to. And this does not make them disadvantaged in any society, even less in today's world. On the contrary, if we decide to stay in the company of someone for the mere fact of not being in solitude, we will not give ourselves the real opportunity to enjoy our loneliness to the fullest.

The importance of our requests must be considered. When we ask the universe for something with true faith, it will always listen to us and help us achieve our goal. The request should be as complete and detailed as possible. For example: a woman wished to be surrounded by money. Her request was granted, and she ended up working in the vault of a bank surrounded by a lot of money. Not being carefully specific with her request to the universe, she was effectively surrounded by a lot of money, but it did not belong to her. Therefore, it is important that what we ask is as detailed and specific as possible. For example: If you would like a smart, educated, tall, friendly man or woman but are not specific with more important qualities that you would like your boyfriend or girlfriend to have, you will start praying. If you are Catholic, maybe you will pray to Our Lady of Guadalupe or to Saint Anthony – the Patron of those in love – to get the ideal boyfriend or girlfriend. If you profess another religion, you will pray in its equivalent to find your partner. However, thanks to all your prayers, a widow/er will appear with all the qualities requested, but with five (5) children you did not want because you were not diligently specific to your request.

When you move to a new city, there are numerous associations you can join to build new relationships/friendships. For example, as newcomer communities.

There, new persons in the area can meet people who are in this same situation. They usually have regular meetings that you might attend. Note: There is a wise adage that says: *You can tell a lady and a gentleman, by the way she or he behaves at the table and at game.* If you are one of the people who gives importance to good manners – learn about the etiquette in your new hometown.

You could also plan a blind date with a family member or friend. Remember that you must be extremely specific with what you want. On one occasion a divorced woman tells a co-worker: "I would love to meet a very polite man. I would rather he was a widower. This way I would not have a problem with any exes; would not mind if he had children, and I also want him to be financially stable." With these details, they made an agreement. The co-worker planned a blind date with one of her single friends who possessed all the features mentioned.

The agreed – to appointment was made on a Saturday with the gentleman chosen by her friend. At 8:00 p.m. she finds herself in a restaurant with a person whose physical features were not compatible with the ones she had imagined. So, she felt a little uncomfortable. However, – thanks to her good education – she disguised her disenchantment. The gentleman got up when he saw her arrive. She approached him and greeted him politely by shaking hands, as it is not appropriate to kiss someone you just met. Throughout the evening, her companion behaved politely and was attentive to every detail to make her feel like a queen. They tasted an exquisite dinner accompanied by a delicious red wine, recommended by the sommelier. However, despite the beautiful night they spent together – as the first impression tells a lot – the woman considered the date unimportant and preferred not to meet this wooer again.

Some believe that having a boyfriend means that we are widely accepted socially. Others associate the couple with a trophy, especially if they are the most beautiful in school, college, or the workplace. There is also the false belief that we are worth more – as a human being – if we are in a relationship. However, it must be considered that there are valuable people who by their own choice are alone – as not in a couple. Similarly, there are also women who boast about saying: "I prefer to undress a drunk than dress saints," which means that they want to marry at all costs forgetting *that it is better to be alone than in bad company.*

If you want to have a relationship that is worth it - the search for that person must be in the right place. If you want a non-smoker or someone who does not like alcoholic beverages, do not go looking for them in a bar. If you want a traditional person with principles like yours, do not look for him or her in a hippie commune. Most likely, you should look in the right places such as groups of friends, who share your lifestyle. If you want to look for a contemporary companion like you, who will see life seriously and be responsible, do not frequent circuses, discotheque, or places for generations younger than yours. It is advisable to visit museums, libraries, art halls, theater and those important events of the city where you live. Join groups where there is an affinity with your way of being or seeing life.

In the old days, women did not want to be alone because socially, and even in certain places or events, an accompanied woman looked better than one that was alone. It is worth mentioning, that there are still places in the world where it is inappropriate for ladies to attend a hotel without a companion, sit down to eat in a restaurant without company, or to have an alcoholic drink in a bar. Because there is still a belief – for some – that if this woman is alone it is because she goes on the hunt for a companion or is on the lookout for possible candidates in restaurants, bars, and hotels.

Today, both in the Western world, and in other parts of the world, the female sex has passed this stage. Currently, senior executives and female entrepreneurs have lunch in restaurants alone because they are travelling through a place or a country. They are in the lobby of a busy hotel with their cell phones, their laptops or maybe waiting for a person related to their work without any hassle.

Times have changed and women – without being executives – in addition to restaurants, can also go to parties, a theatre, or the cinema. Likewise, some women even dare to sit at a bar without intending to find a partner. They only do so with the intention of enjoying a delicious cocktail. In these cases, attention should always be paid to clothing, skirt length and behavior so that it avoids sending the wrong signals to the people around you. You can also prevent unpleasant situations – especially in conservative cities or countries as I told you above. In addition, if the lady is distracted by her environment; someone might intentionally put something in her drink and being unaccompanied will not help her.

When you go to a bar it is always recommendable to take care. Keep an eye on whatever drink you are having, whether you are male or female. Likewise, it is not prudent to drive after you have ingested some alcoholic beverages, therefore it is advisable to order a taxi or a reliable service to transport you safely to your destination.

Some men comment, I would like to have an elegant, polite, friendly woman who acts and dresses like a princess, and who has a lot of affinity with my whole family. This sounds nice. But it turns out that by frequently visiting the bar on the corner of the place where they work, one of them ends up getting not the educated and professionally successful executive woman, but a female with doubtful behavior who wears an indecorous wardrobe, with vulgar vocabulary, chewing gum with her mouth open – like other foods – and eats with her arms on the table, etc. Then, he would like to take her to dinner at his grandmother's house, who is a lady with excellent manners and who possesses the right behavior for every occasion. However, the likelihood of her being compatible not only with grandma, but also with the mother, the siblings, and the other relatives would be exceptionally low, right? As a result, everyone will end up rejecting the woman and he will call out, as in the films of forbidden love: "They are not going to separate us." He identifies with Richard Gere in the film "Pretty Woman," imagines that his girlfriend is Vivian Ward played by Julia Roberts and simply – for being contrary – he marries her.

There are cases of relationships that start in a bar and end with a couple married for more than fifty years. But the law of probabilities says that it is not very promising and less under these parameters. The reality is that mutual coexistence with this difference in social behavior would not be very pleasant. Planning a future together, they will have children who his wife will not be able to educate, and the rest of the relatives will exclude them from any family event. Subsequently at the time of the divorce – the children will end up in a real nightmare – and this man, within his helplessness, will not know how to explain to his children that this was the mother he chose for them. In this case, it is good to remember Confucius's phrase: "Where there is a good education, there is no distinction of classes." Also, an anecdote from this wise man:

Tzu Chang asked Confucius about Jen – the virtue of virtues. Confucius said, "If you can practice these five things with all the people, you can be called Jen." Tzu Chang asked what they were.

Confucius said, "Courtesy, generosity, honesty, persistence, and kindness. If you are courteous, you will not be disrespected; if you are generous, you will gain everything. If you are honest, people will rely on you. If you are persistent you will get results. If you are kind, you can employ people.

Confucius said he never really saw a fully expressed Jen. Therefore, if we want a more lasting and profound relationship, we must analyze it; you are not going to find a Jen but at least a person with good characteristics that makes your life happier. If you are one of those who likes the best, you probably will not go just anywhere. So, if you are going to pick a restaurant, you will usually investigate whether the one you have chosen – to delight in a good drink or an exquisite dish – has the right conditions. For example: if it is clean, if the staff is friendly, if the food has good presentation and if you have good references... Better yet! However, if you happen to be in the middle of the desert and you find there is only one restaurant, then you will have to adapt to the circumstances. Therefore, your analytical capacity must be present in all aspects of your life – especially when it comes to the issue of love. Also remember the saying, "Tell me who your friends are, and I will tell you who you are." This applies to friendships and to our partner.

We can see that there are people who have traveled the world and have failed to open their minds; and others that have not left their place of origin, and yet they have their mind ready to be filled with adventures and information. The mind – like hot air balloons – works better full (with good information) than empty. When you are looking for your partner, this point – depending on your situation – could also be important and even more so, if the person you are interested in belongs to another culture.

However, in the end, the search for love will depend on the tastes and needs of the moment of each human being. Today, technology could play an important role in finding that special person. However, emotional life has little to do with that vehicle. For new generations, for example, commonly known as millennials, virtual life seems to play a particularly important role. This type of communication is apparently their priority and the search for that specific person could be going out of fashion for a high percentage of this generation. It has been determined that in human behavior, due to the accelerated speed of today, some prefer the freedom and disorder of the virtual world, rather than taking responsibility for integration into the real world.

However, the virtual world weighs on our reality and we have not ceased to belong to planet Earth. Nor have we ceased to be human beings who feel, dream and are excited, right?... So, to find our way to a successful relationship we must contemplate certain aspects, which concern us all sooner or later. At the end of the day, belonging to a certain generation does not absolve us of feeling, of wanting to love and be loved, and of wanting to obtain it with as many tools as possible. It must be considered that being carried away by "falling in love" or the mere desire to check our sexual abilities, will not determine the outcome of a successful and lasting relationship.

There is a phrase from the Bible that says: *Do not give pearls to swine – to pigs*. This wisdom is sharing by many other religions, whether you are Muslim, Buddhism or Jewish – to name a few of the world's religions. In other words, do not give someone else what this person is not going to value: gifts, time, dedication, and even less... your love.

Important points of etiquette to consider in the search for love:

1. *Treat others the way you would like to be treated.*
2. *Do not show up in a house unannounced.*
3. *Be punctual! and say hi! when you walk in.*
4. *The cell phone should not be part of the guests and even less of a couple.*
5. *If you have not invited a person to watch TV, turn it off and enjoy his/her company.*
6. *Do not abuse the hospitality a host provides you, such as opening the refrigerator without permission.*
7. *Being thankful is especially important in human relationships. Remember, it is from well-mannered people to be grateful.*

Chapter *Two*

♥ You must know what you want

"We come to love not to find a perfect person, but to learn to see an imperfect person, perfectly." Sam Keen.

In Chapter One, I have already given you certain ideas of how we can find our ideal partner. You may have already read Gary Chapman's "The 5 Languages of Love" (2013). If you have not, I recommend it if what you expect from your relationship is that it is something permanent and not a simple holiday flirtation. Chapman, tells us that there are five love languages alphabetically:

1. Acts of service
2. Physical touch
3. Quality time
4. Receiving gifts,
5. Words of affirmation

Chapman 2013 proposes that each person has a special way of receiving or appreciating love. Knowing this, will help them be more assertive to love their partner.

If you want to get a prince you must start by being a princess – and vice versa – if he wants to get a princess, he must start by being a prince. I refer to the following: we often comment that our partner must be educated, have manners, and that he or she should know how to behave according to every circumstance that is presented in our lives. However, how could you ask for this if you do not own it first? On the other hand, if we do appreciate good manners and practice them, we can expect the same from our companion. Do not settle for a person who has inappropriate behavior. It is human to sometimes be wrong... it is normal. We can even make a list of all our mistakes when we start dating. However, while some of those misadventures may be even funny, others may not be so funny – and inadvertently – you could get your gentleman or damsel to run away from you. He or she could even change his or her address and phone number to simply avoid you and disappear.

For example, when – in the novels – the rich man marries the poor illiterate flower-street saleswoman and takes her to live in his palace, they do not tell us what happened after the honeymoon or if they came to fulfill at least their paper weddings – that is to say, their first year of marriage. We can also analyze that, according to Cinderella's history, the prince was impressed by her beauty and fell in love at first sight. However, they do not mention that in the true Cinderella story, she came from a wealthy family, and that she was the daughter of highly educated people. It was not until her father's death that the stepmother treated her as a domestic servant or as a slave.

Cinderella, despite having performed the trades of the house or suffered the humiliations that her stepmother and stepsisters imposed on her, was never described as a person without manners. On the contrary, she was a very friendly, polite and helpful young woman with all those who knew her, including all the animals that accompanied her. It was probably because of the family principles she received since she was born. It is worth mentioning that, although all this is a fantasy brought to the cinema by Walt Disney; in real life, the more important thing is that the more similar our principles, values, education and our approach to seeing life, the easier our dealings with the people we choose from friends and especially with the person we choose to share our lives.

When I talk to you about the importance of education, I am not just talking about academic instruction, I am referring to etiquette, good manners, and knowing how to behave in different circumstances. There is a well-known saying in Spanish that says: *man is like the bear, the uglier he is, the more handsome he is.* A high percentage of women are not attracted to bears or to live in caves with men whose way of acting and their mentality reflect cave-era behavior. Certainly, there are women who like sweaty almost naked – or in Adam's costume- men dancing in front of them. On the other hand, others – although they like to see the muscular bodies of some men - prefer them to dress elegantly or use the appropriate *dress code* on each occasion. And even if the weather is summer, and they have a good body, they like to see them dressed according either at a formal or informal table, when they sit for lunch as this is considered a showing of respect to all diners. It must be acknowledged that there is no accounting for taste. However, knowing what you like and what you

want is only up to you. Let us remember that the result we get will respond to our behavior. In addition, it should be noted that what works for someone, will not necessarily work for everyone.

I would like to share with you a real-life case in relation to those men who are short of manners. A woman started dating a man who, if we rated his physical attractiveness from one to ten, would get a rating of ten. She felt extremely excited until the day he invited her to the beach. The food they brought for the picnic included some fried chicken from a fast food chain. At the time of eating, this man behaved like a person without manners. He devoured the chicken pieces in an aggressively caveman way. He also chatted with his mouth open as he chewed every bite and did not use the napkin to groom his fat-stricken hands with food residue. This character literally sucked his fingers one by one. At that time, the woman suffered a severe disappointment due to the behavior of this individual, because he did not behave like a gentleman. After this devastating experience, she knew that this person was never going to be a good companion at the formal dinners that she – for her executive, social and family level – was used to attending. When she said goodbye, she canceled an appointment that she previously scheduled with this person.

Unfortunately, our behavior and manners influence our decisions, and when we misbehave the impression reflected is very unfavorable. In this case he was surprised and did not understand why that woman did not want to go out with him again. There is an appropriate saying in Spanish, *do not get dressed because you are not going*. In other words, the rejection in this case had nothing to do with the financial position, nor with his physical appearance; it was due to his rudeness, and his lack of good manners. Days later she began dating a fellow college classmate, not so handsome, but with excellent behavior and wonderful manners. Later, they fell in love and formed a happy family. I would like to point out that chicken, on the table, is eaten with cutlery. If in a casual setting you must eat chicken with your hands, do it as little barbaric as you can.

According to the famous writer Manuel Antonio Carreño, known for his "Manual of Urbanity and Good Manners for young people of both sexes", it is recommended that in a formal meal or where we are invited as guests, the hosts are the ones to establish the guidelines of behavior at the table. That is, if they eat with oriental chopsticks, with cutlery, or with their hands, it is suggested that this is how you should do it. It is worth noting that, if the hosts perform some misplaced behavior such as: placing their elbow on the table, sucking their fingers or wiping their hands with the tablecloth, you are not obliged to do so, because this is not appropriate.

In the event that a gentleman invites a beautiful lady to a date, that is dressed in fashionable clothes, and scented with an exquisite fragrance, but her behavior at the table and when she accompanies him to social events, is not up to the gentleman's manners; after that day, the charm will be over. A professional and educated gentleman will not ask her out again, even if he is chemically attracted to her.

Just as when they are going to hire us for a job, they invite us to eat to evaluate how we do it, when we start dating someone we will also be evaluated. Take care of the small details such as grasping the glass of wine by the stem, in this way its contents will not heat up. Unless it has brandy or cognac whose drink is best enjoyed if we "embrace" the glass. The napkin will usually

be seen on the left side of the main course, on the plate, or also – in some cases – will be placed –like in some countries in Europe – on its right side but not inside a glass.

Women now have the advantage that society is not as strict as in past times. Several decades ago, even when you were invited to dinner or a movie theater, you needed a chaperone. Today it is normally accepted that the woman goes out alone with a gentleman. Do not rush it. Remember that freedom does not mean debauchery. Freedom entails respect and responsibility for our actions. Debauchery, on the other hand, denotes disrespect to the norms and values of society. You must know how to make use of freedom.

Do not be desperate to get a partner. Whether you meet someone in your own home because they are friends of the family, studying at school or college, at work, or under any other circumstances, take your time. As I mentioned in Chapter One, it is recommended that we see the relationship that we are starting as if we were reading a book and with the best use of our analytical capacity in relation to what is best for us.

It is also worth mentioning that there are several sayings about the fictitious interest that some men and women can demonstrate for the sole purpose of having sex and nothing else. On one occasion, a well-known and blissful gynecologist commented on the following in relation to the thinking of some men: *promises, promises until I lay down, after I laid down, forget what was promised.* Does not sound fair to you, does it? But this is the mentality of some men whose goal is simply to satiate their sexual instincts. It will be up to you as an intelligent woman to evaluate what you want, and what you want to get from a relationship. No one else will do it for you. These situations usually occur for both sexes.

Also, there are women who insinuate themselves, and a strategic plan of conquest is drawn up with the sole purpose of making the man they are dating believe, that what they are feeling is true love, when really all they want is to spend a good night, make short trips for free; and then *if I see you, I do not remember you.*

You can read several books like this, where it is mentioned: I am not the kind of girl you can call when you are lonely. Just like when you go out with several people, you will learn a little bit about each one. However, the most important thing I would like to point out is that, to have a pleasurable and serious relationship, both parties must be tuned to the same frequency. It may be that the charm that comes from behavior may excite the person to want to continue sharing their time with the lady or gentleman, but both must be ready for the relationship. Because, for example, if that gentleman is twenty-five years old at the time, and he needs ten more years to finish several medical specialties he wants to study before he marries, and the girl is one of those who wishes to be a mother before her thirties – having the same age – it will be up to them to make a decision about it. Such a decision by the woman would be focused on the desire to continue in the same boat of the future doctor with various specializations or get off this boat in time. Another example would be a guy in love who already wants to formalize the relationship and have the ideal home with children and even a dog with a girl, who wants to give herself more time before formalizing the relationship. In this case, they would not be on the same frequency, and this relationship would eventually end.

We need to understand why we should always behave with good manners. It is advisable that from the beginning, there is a good suggestion to use those magic words that we all know, such as: good morning, good afternoon, good evening, bye, thank you, you are welcome, please, good appetite, excuse me and forgive me – among others.

And if you are a gentleman who made any serious mistake, maybe you can ask for forgiveness by sending her a nice flower arrangement with a beautiful card, or you can offer her a serenade accompanied by musicians or mariachis. You will be able to prove your singing skills. If

it is the lady who commits an offense, it is not recommended that she brings a serenade to a gentleman – depending on the culture or the country where she lives – this would not be well seen. She could even be labeled as having low self-esteem, or the people around them can make a video that will get a lot of viewers in social media. Although she knows she made a serious mistake, it is advisable to apologize at the time, and if he does not acknowledge her sincere words – as they are still at the stage of getting to know each other – she can do nothing but give him time.

Because, again – depending of the culture and/or a country – whether we like it or not, when it is the man who pushes, they call him in love, and the people – around him who hear his serenade – will side with him, and even advise the girl to give him a second chance, if what he did was not very relevant. On the other hand, if the woman is the one who insists, she will not be well seen, and some persons will recommend the guy that it is better for him to end his relationship. Since they could label the woman as complicated or worse, even if she is a good girl who at a bad time made a mistake.

Anecdote

I know the case of a young Swedish woman with many attributes. She was an excellent person with a great human quality who one day – by mistake – replied to her Moroccan boyfriend with a few misplaced words. Unfortunately, after a beautiful relationship and the sincere love that both had shown each other for some time, the relationship was over.

After the young woman uttered the high-meaning words, the boy felt that his heart broke into pieces in that instant, thinking that no woman could ever treat him in such a rude way, even less his fiancée on the eve of their marriage.

The wedding was cancelled even though the girl tried to apologize in a thousand ways, but she was unjustly not heard. It is worth mentioning that in countries where submission and respect for man are notable, such situations are viewed more seriously than in Western countries.

Remember: Whatever country you are in, in all relationships there must be respect and even more so in these relationships. It is recommended that before you speak, you think, use the right words, and even more so when you are upset.

Although chivalry should never go out of style, I remember the time, when it became fashionable among young, and not so young, women, that they did not like the men to be chivalrous with them. They did not see the courtesy of a gentleman to open the car door for her with good eyes. The argument was, "I am not invalid, and I can open the door and carry my packages." Around 1973, almost half a century ago, a book appeared by an Argentine lady of German origin, Esther Vilar, entitled: "The Manipulated Man", where it was implied that men were manipulated by women. I like the author's stance on intellectual equality between men and women. And even more so in my circumstances, when I chose – in the same decade – a career considered for men, as engineering was. In my case, I studied civil engineering at the suggestion of my architect father. Since my dad noticed since I was a child, I loved numbers. I liked to assemble and disassemble electrical appliances and by twelve, I could install a fixture on the ceiling by myself.

I loved subjects like math, physics, and chemistry – which was not quite common among girls. I can mention that I also played with my beloved dolls. I acknowledge this because we tend to believe that if a boy plays dolls with girls, he is going to be gay, and that if girls play assembling electric carts or study careers where men predominate, they could be lesbians. And this is not always true. When I started my civil engineering career, the percentage was that out of one hundred students enrolled in the career, only ten were women. At the end, I was the only one in the civil engineering class at the university where I graduated in the United States. The most interesting thing about this time of my life, with respect for male and female relationships, was knowing the way men behave when they are alone. It was a great experience for me to know what my classmates really thought about us women.

Today women are still underrepresented in this field worldwide, and this has nothing to do with women engineers liking being treated like ladies by their colleagues or by their husbands. I never felt like a man even though in my classes in college or in some construction site, I was often the only woman present. On the contrary, I feel incredibly happy being feminine. I love it when a gentleman – Thank God! there are many still – opens the door for me and more if my hands are full of things. It is nice when we are on a plane trying to get our hand luggage into the overhead compartment traveling alone, and it is amazing to find a gentleman who kindly helps us put that briefcase in the right place. One gives thanks and breathes with a feeling of joy, noticing that there are still many polite and kind men in the world.

On the other hand, what woman does not feel flattered when a gentleman treats her and makes her feel like a queen? or when we hear a beautiful compliment from a gentleman. Depending on who, we may dislike it – this gesture coming from a coworker, can be called sexual harassment –, but if our lover flatters us with beautiful words at an appropriate time, we can notice the importance that words cause in us. I believe that in general, women like to be cared for, and that this has nothing to do with the *machismo* that boasts a supremacy of men over women. I believe in intellectual equality, so I cannot agree with *machismo*, but yes! with chivalry. These are different issues. Moreover, I also do not approve comments such as: "All women are equal"; "all women are bad"; "all men are equal"; or "all men are bad." I tell you that in my life, I have met good and bad people of both sexes. And ironically, I have met male and/or female twins who, despite being physically equal, are inwardly widely different.

When one gets used to the good treatment by his partner from the beginning, the moment the relation moves to another stage – they get married or get pregnant – the woman will need more care and if her partner was already used to lavishing them, it always will be better – for both – to do it correctly. It is as if they dine daily at their home table like a lady and a gentleman respecting the rules of good education. And suppose that one day you are invited to a formal dinner, you will notice that there are several knives on your right side and several forks on your left side of the plate. As a result, they will know how to use them correctly – from the outside in – they will not feel like the actors in a theatre, and they will do so in a very natural way.

They will sit upright on the table, placing the napkin on their lap, bringing the fork to their mouth, and not lowering their head to the plate. We are not putting our left arm on the table. In addition, they will know that their bread plate is the one on their left side, and they will not take the bread from the dish on their right side – which corresponds to the other diner. A good treatment rules from the beginning with respect, setting the correct pattern of the relationship. We cannot allow ourselves to be mistreated or treated as if we were objects. As good as people are, if they get used to a disrespectful type of relationship, it will be complicated and difficult, wanting a better interaction with the passing of time.

If since we started dating, our partner is friendly and opens the door of a car and it agrees with us, the moment the relationship progresses, and may even commit, get engaged, get married and become pregnant, this respectful treatment will be more familiar to them. However, if the woman feels too independent, and does not like to be helped, what happens when she needs her partner to take care of her when she is sick or expecting a baby? She cannot expect that her companion will learn at that time, that he must open the car door for her, that he must take care of her because she can no longer cope with the weight of the things she carries; and that he must also take care of the new family member, because these cares will be necessary. By this I do not mean that women must take the attitude of invalid and be exaggerated in their requirements. Therefore, it is advisable to do it properly from the time they start dating their partner. As with the example of sitting down to dinner properly at the table, it should not be practiced only on special occasions, but always. When presenting a thank you card according to the

occasion, when we wrap a gift properly, when serving a nice drink or a plate of food, by bringing some beautiful flowers to a damsel, and in many other small gestures. Because at the bottom of the situation, *the small details make the big differences*. This saying can be applied to everything we do in our lives.

Important points of etiquette for a good coexistence when we look for what we want:

1. *In the United States, you can say "Bon Appétit!" or "Enjoy your meal!".*
2. *If we are eating – neither the elbows nor the forearm should be placed on the table.*
3. *Cutlery is used from the outside in. The knives and the soup spoon go to your right side and the forks on your left side.*
4. *Cutlery is not placed as oars on the sides of the plate, nor is they used to target something or someone.*
5. *Do not suck your fingers. It is not well seen and even less at the table.*
6. *Pets are not fed while eating with other people, even with family.*
7. *The topics of conversation at the table should be nice. Avoid unsuitable ones, such as money, medical procedures, or problems of any kind. The issue of sex, religion or politics is ideal for another time, when the two of you are alone, and thus both will be able to know the other's views on these matters. Take care of the tone of voice and that the way you laugh is not vulgar or exaggerated.*

Chapter *Three*

♥ The beginning of a relationship

"The proof of love is in the works. Where love exists, great things are done and when they are no longer done it ceases to exist." Saint Gregory the Great.

There are monogamous animals such as parakeets, penguins, seahorses, famous lovebirds and swans, who choose their partner for life. In the case of us humans, sometimes we are not as faithful as these species of animals. However, we have the enormous advantage that we can be more analytical. One of the most important points to consider, is that our potential boyfriend or girlfriend is free of commitments.

Some people start by writing down on paper the most relevant points they would like their partners to have. They also write down the important life plans they have. In this way, they clearly define their priorities before entering a couple's relationship. If religion is a primary factor in your existence, it is advisable for your partner to practice the same doctrine, or at least not be uncompromising with the beliefs you profess. Perhaps by continuing the relationship, one of the two could assimilate the faith of the other, although this does not often happen. No one can guarantee it. That is why it is recommended to pay attention to that popular saying that it is, *birds of each feather flock together.*

Since I love number seven (7), I will list the following possible important points you might consider at the beginning of your relationship. Maybe you will have your favorites or essentials that are not on this list. It is just to help you with a few examples:

1. Be a gentleman or a lady - that is polite, classy, and educated.
2. That he or she has values, principles, and human quality.
3. May he or she be a single person who loves and respects the true meaning of the family.
4. Always keep your word.
5. Be respectful and honest.
6. Have a promising future because he or she is always being updated personally, academically, and professionally.
7. Since the beginning, he or she will be treated correctly. First as a friend, then as boyfriend or girlfriend, and if the

relationship is the right one, they are going to be engaged and later, husband or wife.

We can also make the list of seven (7) features that completely displease us from a person, for example, such as:

1. A liar.
2. An addict.
3. An egocentric.
4. An aggressive.
5. A *Casanova* or a coquettish woman.
6. A jealous and/or controlling person.
7. A person who hates the opposite sex.

Over time, you will be aware of:

- His or her tastes.
- His or her ideals.
- His or her hobbies.
- His or her favorite foods.
- His or her favorite music.
- If he or she has complexes.
- What is your level of affinity?
- His or her favorite programs.
- Favorite topics of conversation.
- If the person is wasteful or thrifty.
- How he or she is focused on his/her life.
- If he or she has any illnesses or allergies.
- Whether he or she is a hard-working or a slack person.
- If he or she projects his or her misadventures on others.
- If he or she takes care of his or her manners when sitting, standing, and even shaking hands.
- If he or she does not repair damaged items and prefers to buy new ones.

- If he or she leaves the light and the electrical appliances on, the water runs when he or she is not using it.
- If he or she gives a lot of importance to the physical rather than the spiritual, to the point that he or she notices and makes a big deal if you have a wrinkle or gray hair.
- The life plans you have in common (I do not mean you want to get married, because for the first dates it would be hasty).
- If he or she knows the importance of recycling for the future of humanity. Therefore, he or she separates the trash in the right place

First, you can revise all these points to be sure that you agree with them, and if you are making any mistakes, first you must improve as a person yourself before desiring a better behavior from somebody else. Anyway, with this I am not suggesting that you take out your list -you can make one by yourself- on the first day and read it completely to your companion.

At the beginning of the relationship, the theme on the list is like a game and you do not show your hand at the beginning of the game. You take your time and according to the situation -if it is a game of decks- you will select very well the card that you will use at every moment of the game. If there is the halo of mystery, there will be an interest in discovering each other. Those qualities or defects would not affect your relationship. Therefore, it is not advisable to give your body and soul on the first date you have with a possible boyfriend or girlfriend.

In most cases the man is expected to be older than the woman. However, studies such as that of Andrew Francis and Hugo Mialon indicate that while the age difference between men and women is smaller, the divorce rate is also lower.

Likewise, from the experience that life has given me, I can tell you that the age difference between a man and a woman could be seven (7) years or less, regardless of whether it is the man or the woman who is older. With this difference, generational elements such as: music, the way you dance, fashion and even the existential problems of every decade are shared. The age difference they have as a couple is going to be the same as time goes by. I say this because, although it sounds logical, there are people who only grasp reality after several years together, because gray hairs, wrinkles and other indications appear, reminding us that youth is behind us. Especially when disparity is very noticeable.

It also happens that when the age difference is very evident, other situations appear a little more complicated, such as the topics that interest them and even the physical inability to handle certain situations. Like, for example, if I am fifty and my partner is twenty-five years old, it is highly likely that getting on the roller coasters of some amusement park is not in my interest and even causing me physical problems. Although for my young companion this activity is the greatest enjoyment of his life. In addition, there are behaviors that are quite common to their generation and that in previous times were not so notorious. For example, we can see that there are some young people who demand a lot of freedom, respect for their way of acting, their space and their privacy. The unbalanced thing about this issue is that they do not apply the same concept of respect for their non-contemporary adults. I will cite some examples below. Come to the places not respecting the space of others:

- With their cell phones. They plug in anywhere without asking permission. They use them all the time, no matter if they are at a dinner table with their family or in the middle of a meeting.

- The girls place their bags – on the dining table – loaded with the microbes that have been collected by the places where they have previously placed them, such as bathrooms.
- They leave a mess when they visit their parents. But their parents cannot leave a pencil out of place in their homes.
- They do not make their bed as they should.
- They walk into a place without saying hello.
- They use colognes or fragrances so strong that – inadvertently – they pollute the air.
- They do not give importance to good manners, and even sit at a table without a shirt, with dark glasses and/ or with a baseball cap or a hat.
- They do not take care of his/her spelling. They end up writing with spelling horrors, all in lowercase or uppercase without respecting their own names or words that begin with the capital letter. And furthermore, they abuse swearing words in their writings. When receiving a text with those characteristics, it is difficult to decrypt its contents.

They think they know everything and if you give them a comment about it, they are offended. If you are an adult who does not give more importance to this type of details, the generation gap will not affect you.

I would like to mention that Thank God! Not all young people are like this, many are also charming, polite, respectful and with excellent behavior, worthy of admiration.

There is another point that we accept with more tolerance when we are younger, it is what it would be like to deal with the excessive volume of a disco, a concert or a party. However, if both are peers, they will enjoy these circumstances together. It is also not pleasant to accompany your young partner to a social gathering after work, if you are dressed as an executive and the rest of the guests are dressed in denim pants and casual T-shirts. In addition, as the conversation revolves around university studies, you will have in mind the presentation that you should prepare to present on your next trip to Europe. So, you might feel *out of place*. If your girl also nicknames you *Daddy* and physically you look like one; and a guy heard his father call his mother, *Mom* all his life (even if he was younger than his father) and this boy decides to call his companion - older than him - with the same nickname; such couples will not be well understood and only in rare cases will be on their way to a happy future.

When we reach maturity and have already burned several stages of our lives as partygoers, we do not have the vitality or the time – because of our responsibilities – to constantly go out and have fun like the twentysomethings or even those who have not reached even the age of forty.

Therefore, our tastes are quieter. Instead of a crowd, we prefer a group of a few select people. We would like to spend an afternoon with our partner in a park playing guitar. We could watch a sunrise or sunset, spend a night playing cards, go to the theater, a piano bar, enjoy singing in a karaoke place, or just cuddle with our partner watching some TV series at home.

When we decide to start a family and have children – even to educate them – it is also going to be complicated if the age difference is noticeable. Because everyone will see the matter according to the time he lived. For example, we who have several decades of existence, were entertained as children with books, toys, board games, with coloring books and playing outdoors. Unfortunately, in more recent generations, they find it normal to entertain their children for hours with electronics, which is concerning. Ideally, at that age, they will explore the world around them and learn to socialize properly.

When we have over half a century of life or more, it is different to enjoy the grandchildren for a while than to start dealing with our own children. Our energy is not the same. There are girls who love older men because they tend to have more financial stability, and they treat them with a chivalry that some young guys today do not show towards women. There are cases where young women see in these lovers the father figure they did not have at home, because of the divorce of their parents or because they have been raised by single mothers. In first world countries, there are young women from less economically fortunate nations, who marry the elderly hoping that when they die, they will leave them with a good financial pension. We also know that there are exceptions, that there are men with half a century of life who get along wonderfully with their 20-year-old partner and both enjoy their love fully.

If your family and friends have already introduced you to the candidates they had kindly selected because they knew they were people who met the seven (7) essential qualities on your list and yet none of them clicked you right, then I am going to suggest several alternatives where you could meet your potential partner:

- The gym.
- Practicing a sport.
- Language school.
- Walking with your pet.
- At a dance academy.
- Associations for the activity you like.
- Your place of worship.
- Taking a course on a topic of interest to you.
- A social club where sometimes there is a group of bachelors.
- On a cruise, there is a chance to meet new people.
- You can take an organized trip with a tourist agency or by yourself.
- If you like gastronomy, there are places where they teach gourmet food.
- There are single people who like to go to the supermarket after hours and on weekends, to meet prospective partners.
- A company that is engaged in finding a partner for busy singles who do not have time for the aforementioned points.

By browsing the Internet, we can get other ideas, and the best thing is that you have other sites that you can add to this list. If you are new to a city, find out if they have Internations in that locality. And if you can register, you can meet people who, like you, are expats, https://www.internations.org/.

Social media Etiquette:

- *The first rule of good education also applies to the social media tag. Do not do to others, what you do not like to be done to you.*
- *Writing everything in capital letters is considered like you are shouting.*
- *You should not use social media to harm others or to disseminate false information.*
- *Do not give anyone's personal information.*
- *Respond to messages you receive through social media.*
- *You must not use the net to commit felonies.*
- *Use only the programs you are authorized to use.*
- *Remember that uploading to social media can benefit users.*
- *Think about it before submitting the information if there is a possibility of harming the community.*
- *Use the language correctly when you speak and when you write.*
- *Avoid severed, misspelled words and cursing words.*
- *Do not like your own messages. Let others have their opinions on your photo or message. In my opinion, if*

your friends or followers ask you a question, you can answer them or make a comment.

- *Do not abuse hashtags.*
- *Do not vent personal issues on your Facebook, Instagram, or any other social media profile.*
- *Respect other people's bandwidth.*
- *Avoid distasteful jokes that, in addition to consuming space, benefit no one.*
- *Do not abuse the power or benefits you may have.*

You must always demonstrate your good manners in the forums, in the chats, on Twitter, Instagram, Facebook, WhatsApp in the comments you leave anywhere from these or other websites.

Here are several suggestions for you to enjoy with a new friend:

- Bowling.
- Go to the zoo.
- Visit a museum.
- Go to the movies.
- Go to the theater.
- Play board games.
- A picnic in the park.
- Attend a meeting with friends.
- Plan a walk through the city.
- Go to the farmers' market on Saturday.
- Practice or go watch a game of the sport you like.
- If they profess the same religion, you could go to church, the temple, synagogue, or the place where they meet.
- Activities according to the time of year such as shopping together at Christmas.

- Visit the city's special attractions.
- Go to the beach, a lake, the river, the countryside, or the mountain if you have those alternatives near where you reside.
- Activities according to the time of year such as shopping together at Christmas.
- The special activities of the city to see if any would like to go.
- Go to the beach, a lake, the river, the countryside, or the mountain if you have those alternatives near where you reside.

Some of these ideas you will not do at the beginning of your relationship. But as you spend your time together, it is good to know if your new friend enjoys the same things you like. In different situations, you will know different facets of that person and they will realize how they think according to each situation. Keep in mind that there are all kinds of people. Those who open their hearts at once, the ones that are most reserved, those who take the time before saying something about their childhood – or their past – and those who can look charming and be – on the contrary – manipulative, and perverse people when we already

know them best. That is why I recommend you read this book chapter after chapter. Because when you start a book with the last chapter the first ones will not be exciting and may not have the same impact as if you read it the way it has been structured. In fact, a good relationship can be compared to reading a book where if we start to delight page by page, step by step, little by little, we will achieve what is most important – the real connection with the other person.

Sometimes we trust someone who can apparently seem *truly kind* and ends up being an undesirable person. There are cases of cyber gigolos who take advantage of lonely ladies, who believe in the love that these individuals apparently offer and end up making money from them, simply using any excuse to achieve it. Men are also conned by women who act like those Internet gigolos and thus obtain money in an unscrupulous way.

If after a previous review you decide to meet in real life with your cyber acquaintance, it is advisable to tell a family member or friend where you will be, and with whom. I suggest the first date be a short encounter. For example, having a tea or coffee. Thus, if the other person is not to your liking, that is where the relationship ends. If both are excited with the appearance and conversation and want to continue the conversation with a dinner invitation, it means they are on the right track. When we start dating a person and through courtship, they will gradually get to know each other. You are not going to open your mind and heart wide in front of a person you only met a few days ago or maybe a few months ago.

The characteristics that everyone possesses and expects their companion to know will appear in due time through contact, as will their tastes and entertainments. This way you will realize if they can live with the way the other person is and behaves. Let us remember that human beings not only have qualities, we also possess flaws, that will emerge over time. It is good to be clear that the best sign of education a person can show is to control their temper and emotions.

Therefore, our character can be compared to the reins of a horse. If we let him free rein, the horse and temper can be unbridled. We need to analyze our flaws and become aware of those we must and can change.

There are couples who took longer to prepare for the wedding than to make the decision to divorce. It means that if the person possesses the following peculiarities: he is a boxing fan; he is extremely unpunctual; has the same routine every weekend; enjoys spending hours talking on the phone; his dog is inseparable – sleeps with him; likes his partner to have black hair and the person is blonde; he doesn't like to be looked in the eyes when spoken to; walks an hour in the morning and another in the evening; and eats many times a day. Well, none of these details is serious for a tolerant person. However, we must be clear in recognizing which behaviors we can change – for the welfare of both – and which are impossible to accept. For example, if you are into punctuality, you do not like to walk, you do not like dogs, think about it. You may not be entirely compatible. That is why at this stage it is good to analyze the couple and to think about what we like, and what bothers us. Otherwise, you should think about whether it is your own best interest to end the love relationship right now before moving on to the most serious stages of a relationship.

Before holding hands, before you kiss, and before anything else, it is good to know your partner's way of thinking. Imagine that you have a passionate affair with a new acquaintance, and through fate your birth control method failed, and you became pregnant. And because you disapprove of abortion, you do not consider it an alternative. With the baby on the way, you realize that the child's father has a list of flaws and has a horrendous past. Then how are you going to explain to your child that he was the father you chose for him or her? And if you're a gentleman and you decide to have a passionate affair with a woman of a different intellectual level or different principles than yours, remember that if she gets pregnant and decides to have the baby that person is going to be your child's mother. She will be the one to dictate the guidelines of education and instruction that child will receive.

There are married people whose eyes shine when they tell us their love story and relive that magical moment that is the remembrance of that feeling of love that united them. Some say that from the first moment they knew they got the right person. Others had a friendly relationship until cupid targeted them to turn friendship into a beautiful love attraction. I also know of stories of couples where the perseverance of a lover achieves, with small and great details, through polite behavior, the love of the other person. For example, I know the case of a couple who started out as great friends. They supported each other, loved to share their time together, and – above all – acted selflessly with each other. They rejoiced every time the gentleman would give the lady an invitation and say, "Can I come by your house? Shall we go to the movies? Shall we have dinner together? She also corresponded to invitations including him at family dinners. Sometimes, they would pay tickets to a movie, sit in a good restaurant or just share meals at home. Love appeared, because they gradually realized that they had many affinities, and that they were attracted in such a way that they are now married for several years. This has been a huge joy for them, their friends, and their family. Stories of this kind are real, and some have been a source of inspiration for romantic films.

A wonderful thing about this stage is the enjoyment; delighting in an *hors d'oeuvre* and, if it is seafood, making sure that your partner is not allergic. Enjoying a good glass of wine or just something refreshing. In this way through their tastes they can begin to read each other, and likewise, begin to know the other's book of life. It is the stage where we will discuss different topics, like what we think of La Paz (means peace in English), the capital city of Bolivia. One could also talk about peace and even wars. About our last trip; nature; about famous writers or famous men; UFOs; about past civilizations. In addition to the tastes, flavors and colors of each.

It is like you are getting to participate in these programs where only the man or the woman is taken away and they ask him or her questions about his/her partner's tastes. The man or the woman would give his/her answers and when the gentleman or the lady returns to the studio – and they ask the same questions – sometimes those answers do not coincide despite having several years of marriage. If from the beginning you care about getting to truly know each other, you will be able to respond correctly. You will also be able to talk about topics vetoed at social gatherings such as politics, religion, sports, money and even sex – but the two alone – giving free rein to these and many other issues.

Remember that creativity is fabulous and highly appreciated in today's life. Therefore, use it when planning exclusive meetings for you two or when including others. For a couple who is starting out, it is advisable not only to share by yourselves but also with family and friends. Several eyes see more than one, and if you are going to be the other's life partner, it will be fabulous if you gradually join your family circles, and your groups of friends. In addition, you will notice if that person is one of those who integrates or one of those who rejects your family or friends, and even ends up criticizing them, which is not acceptable. However, as unfortunately a large majority of families would not win the Family of the Year award, it is preferable to gradually touch on the delicate themes. Of course, it does not go so far as to be already engaged and to completely ignore everything related to your future husband's family.

There are cases that go to the extreme where the couple married, and they do not know if the parents of the other are alive. What is your husband's true work, even if they do not belong to a secret service in your country? They do not know who their childhood friends are or who they meet regularly. Others who wear contact lenses and get up before their partner does to wear them without their life partner noticing. There are men who have never seen their wife without makeup, as there are women who get up in the early hours to beautify herself before her husband wakes up, and always sees her flawless. I think that one must be natural with those who share our existence and get to know their partner as completely as possible and under different situations. However, education, no matter how self-assured you are, should not be neglected, and even less disappear.

There are rare cases of Love at First Sight, but the rest of the great loves take their period to flourish. And if the time spent together is fun and we notice that there is empathy and other feelings, like the beginning of a loving relationship arise then, we will continue to walk paths together; and agree on a new date, another and many others.

Anecdote

A highly cultured woman focused on her work after her divorce. Being a pediatrician, very dedicated to her profession, prevented her from having a romantic relationship, and her romantic life was always in the background. One of her sisters – to make a little joke, knowing her seriousness – signed her up for a couple's search website, completing her profile. When she starts receiving messages, she learns of the joke her sister had planned for her. She continued with her pace of life and one day, one of those messages caught her eye. Since it came from a gentleman who through his writing demonstrated his good education and, in his message, invited her to have tea in a beautiful place.

The mutual pleasure that they received from their companionship was such that they went on to having dinner together, and from that day the relationship grew until it took them to City Hall. The great thing about it is that from the first moment this gentleman was so struck by his companion that every day – on the way to his work – he placed the radio station in Spanish. Because as a Canadian, his language was English. He had also learned French from his parents and for his travels to Paris for work matters as a financial consultant. He felt motivated to learn Spanish, which he achieved, and that was a great advantage for him to be able to integrate into her family. In addition, not only did he learn the language, but also read about culture, music, and enjoy the gastronomy of his Argentinian girlfriend who, as I mentioned, ended up being his wife.

I can conclude this chapter by commenting that by making

the correct use of caution and taking reasonable time, a relationship that begins by using a web page by a partner search portal - sometimes - could work positively.

Important Etiquette Points for the beginning of a good relationship:

1. *Drive politely with respect for traffic signs.*
2. *A gentleman does not honk his horn when he goes to pick up a lady, he gets out to get her. Only in extreme or pre-agreed cases, you can call out to get them.*
3. *Commonly used sport caps, berets, or hats are not appropriate when entering an office or home and even less when sitting at the table.*
4. *Sunglasses are used outdoors, not inside a property and even less if you are talking to someone. It is only justified if the person has a prescription.*
5. *Your purse should not be placed on the table or on the kitchen counter. They are full of germs.*
6. *Do not confuse chivalry with machismo.*
7. *A beautiful compliment is always welcome and more during the stage of the conquest.*

Chapter *Four*

♥ Still, not a kiss...

"Don't ever forget that the first kiss is given with the eyes, not with the lips." Tristan Bernard

As we still do not know each other well, and we are at the stage of knowing each other's minds before becoming aware of being in love, we continue in the stage of only sharing pleasant moments. If your companion shows that he or she insists on kissing, touching, and precipitating the situation, you can already realize that he or she is not on the same frequency as you.

This is where you are going to wonder why I am still asking you to be a little patient with the kiss. Because you would not give your car steering wheel to a person you do not know how they drive, if they have a good car record, if they don't have a driver's license, or if their driving is irresponsible. So, if you must be so careful to ask a potential driver of your car, would not you ask a lot of questions to a being who is going to be involved with your personal life? A lot of girls get complicated in a relationship and they only know they like the guy. Because sometimes they do not even know his full name. And they end up not only kissing but having even sex. Sounds like a movie, doesn't it?

I have seen several cases and I will mention two. One of the cases occurred at the University of Massachusetts where three students shared a dormitory. Two of the classmates were girls focused on their studies, and the other was a party girl. I will call this girl Laura. One day, Laura came super worried in the room because she was afraid, she had become pregnant. But what worried her the most was that that night she had had sex with three different boys from college and did not remember their names. Unfortunately, although her behavior was not the most decorous, Laura did not charge for what she did or was a "bad girl". She was just a poorly advised young student who did not know better, to whom her mother had given birth control pills, and she – in her ignorance – believed her body was an amusement park. She naively thought that what she was doing would have no consequences because – in her mind – her birth control pills would take care of her protection. Until that time when she thought she was pregnant. Which was – thank God – untrue. What I can tell you is that the scare she received was enormous and set her to reconsider the way she behaved.

A worse case than this was that of a girl in Mexico named Maria, who thought she knew her partner and after a year dating dared to have sex with him. Getting pregnant. Unfortunately, the future father, upon learning of this new irresponsibly disappeared from her life. She courageously, for her religious and family principles, ruled out the possibility of an abortion. The seriousness of this situation was that in the second year of this baby's existence he was diagnosed with an illness, and the girl had no idea how to respond to doctors when they asked questions about the family history of the boy's father. For which reason Maria could only answer questions that corresponded to her family's record. Because of Maria's prayers and her great faith in God, in the Virgin of Guadalupe, and in all the angels of heaven, the child was saved and today he is a healthy man and a good professional. The father never cared about him. She had an excellent mother who, at the end of her professional career as a psychologist specializing in human resources, devoted herself body and soul to raising her child. I tell you all this so that you understand that it is a gamble to expose ourselves to a situation before knowing our companion well, with the great possibility of not always succeeding in the situation.

Today, where our media has expanded, we must consider the great influence of social media, in addition to the possibility it provides of doing a little research on those with which we want to get involved. Just being familiar with it, not saturating it with excessive likes and too many hearts that will impel it, unless when they get to know each other better, they are both fascinated by that kind of virtual flirtation. By the time you arrive at this chapter, you have already been through the stage of defining what you would like to obtain from your partner. You have already made your list of the main features you would like your ideal partner to have. You have started dating and talking about various topics to get to know each other. Untitled yet, as simple friends. At this stage there is much to discuss about the possible lover. So far you know if he knows the magic words, and if he uses them properly.

We also know that he has a good education in general. That, if for us to have an educated person by our side is a priority, we have been ruling out those uneducated people and we already have at our side a person who knows how to behave like a gentleman or a lady. And – in this way – you are not going to have to give him an intensive course with guaranteed results if you decide to get married.

You will also have noticed his level of splendidness. Remember that selfless giving is a sign of love. It is an incredibly beautiful gesture because it reveals a generous heart. Gifts can be small details – they do not have to be expensive. For example, they could be flowers that the gentleman gives to the lady with an odd number of flowers indicating that the other flower is the beautiful lady who receives the floral bouquet. It could also be a movie ticket or a dinner out, a dessert that the loved one likes. Simply nice details that will bring you closer together every day.

- We will discuss his behavior with you. You may want to ask yourself the following questions:
- Is he polite?
- Does he express himself correctly?
- Does he treat your parents, family, friends, or employees well?
- Does he dress according to each occasion?
- Do you feel comfortable introducing him to others?
- Does he ridicule you in front of others and can discuss private issues at a social gathering?
- Does he go out with you and keep looking at other women or men, depending on his sexual preference?
- Does he constantly compare you to family members, friends, or others?
- Does he comment on your private life or personal data?

- Does he treat you like an object and act out romantic scenes in public?
- Does he respect your time together, or does he focus on his cell phone or make calls during the two or more hours you are together?
- Does he put his fingers in unsuitable places like his nose, ears, or mouth?
- Does he speak ill of his past relationships and share details of his pre-your love life?
- Does he have a reputation for being aggressive? To the point of hitting someone.
- Socially, does he want to keep you from advancing?
- Does he/she respect your individuality?
- Is he / she possessive, jealous, or dominant?
- Is he/she vindictive?
- Is he / she spiteful?
- Does he want to know the passwords for your social networks and read the messages you receive?
- Does he consider that the woman is inferior to the man or vice versa?
- Does he dismiss and put negative titles on people?
- Is he making fun of you in front of family or friends? Or do you allow him to do it?
- Does he see you above him/her, beneath or next to him?
- Does he promise to do something, and not follow through?
- He leaves everything half done.
- He blames everything that happens on others.
- Do you think he is perfect?
- He does not transmit peace. On the contrary, does he keep you in check?
- Does he love arguing and taking the opposite side?

- Do not use your partner as your mental dumpster.
- Does he have characteristics of a person with behavioral disorder?

I ask you all these questions because many people who want to feel accepted and/or loved, do not notice these details until they are sexually involved with a perfect stranger. Who could hurt them and even steal while they sleep – as it has happened to people – when a crazy one-night stand ended in an absolute nightmare?

There are men and women who place more importance on physical contact or caresses. Therefore, this long-awaited kiss must take place when it is possible for you to assume the exchange of microbes, bacteria, virus (some very dangerous like coronavirus), the energies in common, and everything that involves the decision of physical contact. You will also notice how your spiritual part is involved in these situations.

In human relationships, empathy between the couple plays an important role in us having successful relationships. We will not pester our partner with an overload of messages, photos, or phone calls. It is good to enjoy TV programming when we are alone. Since it is interesting to be up to date on political issues, be aware of current news or issues you know are fashionable, as well as other topics that are to your liking. But do not turn on the TV when someone is visiting at home unless you have come together for this purpose. For example, to see together a political debate, a sport and even a beauty contest.

On one occasion a friend who worked for a transnational company, in one of the countries where she was appointed to a managerial position, met an interesting person. At first, she had already made his list of the important points she expected in her next relationship. I will mention some of them: she wanted him to be polite and to have class (this point is always recommended on the list). That he was not a fan of watching sports on television (fanaticism "per se" is not recommended); that he liked to enjoy them live in a stadium, but not to see them by other means; that he liked exotic foods; that he was a cultured person; that he was in her age group; that they agree on the way they see life; that he tackles problems without losing control (scenes from movies in which he or the protagonist smashes a place in a moment of fury are not pleasant in real life). And finally, that he liked the same style of music as she did. The suitor possessed all these qualities, but she could make a long list of details that were not suitable for the lifestyle of a good couple. Starting with inappropriate behavior that could sometimes be perceived, combined with the inflexibility of his vision regarding globalization. He only liked his country, mocked my friend's accent and taking him out of his comfort zone, terrified him. Thank God! that the situation only played out in several outings to dinner or to a cinema, to share with friends and family, and after that... they separated, never to see each other again.

Today, the reality for many human beings is that we do not belong, I include myself, somewhere in particular because, for reasons of marriage, work, or studies, we have had to live in different countries of the globe. For these types of people, it is sometimes easier to relate to individuals who are part of this lifestyle. In my case, after touring more than a hundred cities and living in more than ten different places on the terrestrial sphere, I have concluded that it is better to add rather than to subtract. It should be about adding the positive that each person, situation, or civilization can offer you; even more, when your partner belongs to another culture.

The good thing about globalization is that it enriches us

intellectually and opens more possibilities in life. In addition, today more than in previous times of humanity, we can visualize the entire terrestrial sphere and enjoy it through travel, music, taste the wide variety of dishes that exist in international gastronomy, share with individuals' different idiosyncrasies from other parts of the world, where we will notice that in other countries – the same situation is handled in another way. And if it is about employment, big globalized companies open possibilities for you to work locally or internationally. What is interesting is that, if it is newlyweds, who have the situation that they move to another country for work reasons, the experience of facing adaptation together in their new place of residence, can unite them as a couple.

Sometimes without having to travel physically, we can connect with another country or culture by visiting a foreign food restaurant, watching international films, participating in festivals in a country like Oktoberfest – the one by the German Club in Mexico City is excellent – and having friends from other places on the planet. And as a complement, we can learn to dance rhythms that come from other places on the planet, different from the one we are usually used to.

On dancing – to the young people I recommend – that, if they do not know how to dance, take a course if necessary; and if it can be with her boyfriend or his girlfriend, even better. Because one of the most beautiful sensations a couple can experience is twirling together on a dance floor or in the living room of their house, getting carried away by the melody of a song. On one occasion I heard a phrase that said something like this: dancing with your partner, it is like making love standing up. Just like the first time they were sexually together and not very coordinated, the same could happen the first time they danced together. But if you are both on the same frequency, you will notice that over time you will gradually manage to do it more harmoniously. It is applicable to both conditions, both when dancing and making love, as this is the ideal goal in both situations.

Feel the love correctly, – no deal in love – it is advisable to keep our feet on the ground. If you live in Miami and you're going to choose a coat to travel to Canada in the middle of winter, you should take the time to look for that coat that meets the conditions that are important to you. As well as the material with which it is made; the color that suits you; the length of the coat according to your height; the cost of the coat tailored to your budget – and most importantly – that it is comfortable. The same goes for that lady or gentleman who will accompany you on a ride to a specific place and then become the companion of the journey of your life.

Excerpts from the Poem of Andrés Eloy Blanco

Liking vs Loving

I am dying to ask you if it is
the same or if it is different
loving and liking, and if it is
true that I love you and you
like me.

Loving and liking to become
equal when you put them as
a couple, the one that likes
and the one that loves.

But it just does not equal out. They say that liking ends and loving is endless; love is until death and liking until you forget.

Liking is not loving. Loving there is time to love it all: God, your partner, the world touches the surface and the deep end and love the town's child like the child from the husband. Is loving for one only and loving for all?

No; loving is loving, and loving is like loving two ways: one like God's sons and Like God, only one. They say that loving does not hurt where liking leaves a mark.

Liking is lust and loving is servitude; liking fills up corners. loving fills up journeys; liking you have a good time loving you have a child.

Loving is with the lights on; liking, with it off; in loving there is more showing off in liking there is more fighting.

It is not sleeping at night It is not seeing the sun in the day Is loving without leaving enough space for God's love.

Is having your heart safely in your hands and when she comes, just feel our hands opening.

Is having woken up without being able to explain,
how without having slept we could have dreamed.

All of this is liking and loving,
and loving is even more,
because loving is the happiness of creating yourself and others.

There is no man that can surpass the version of a man who is loved by a woman and there is no woman as beautiful and there is no woman as pure like the woman who is in the man's thoughts.

Therefore, while I am loving you if with one love, I like you with the other one I am creating you. But loving's creation does not stop there, and it creates a better world for those who do not even have one.

Loving is loving luckily that when you measure it you.

And in loving: The Greatest, and in liking: the deep it is

And just like this, love is a gesture that leaves our hands for human services and looking for justice.

Loving is better liking, and if you try to measure it, it turns out that love is wider than life.
Find that love is longer than death,
that something of what we are liking touches the word.

I really like that poem which gives us an idea of what true love is. For a successful couple's relationship, I would add Antoine De Saint-Exupéry's famous phrase: "Love is not looking at each other but both looking in the same direction." It is no use spending hours looking at each other if our eyes to the future are focused on two different goals - and sometimes even in opposite directions. Take your time to find that ideal partner. No matter how much pressure society imposes on you. Especially if you are a woman, do not get married because you walk out of the way or run away from your parents' house. There are family and friends who enjoy asking bachelors with some insistence: Do you have a boyfriend or a girlfriend? When will you get married? Making bachelors uncomfortable and sometimes causing them to precipitate into inadequate decision-making. Remember that the family is the foundation of society, and just as when a house is to be built it must be built on a good foundation, also, in forming a home, we must base it on a good relationship.

Although in many places good behavior becomes obvious through its absence, I think this basic information can help you notice the right or wrong behavior of the person we are meeting. Just as in board games and in sports there are rules to know the proper way to participate, we can also take advantage of this circumstance to notice the attitude, which you have in a game. Let us remember the saying: *the gentleman and the lady are known at the table and in the game*. That is, if we know the rules to follow in the society where we develop, our social coexistence will be much more pleasant.

As they say a picture speaks more loudly than words.

According to your perception, what does this man transmit through his gaze? And what does a woman transmit through her body language?

Important Etiquette Points when there is still no kiss...

1. "Fashion, what suits you" and perfume or cologne should be used discreetly.
2. Even if you are on the beach if you are going to sit down and eat at a table, put on a shirt. And if you are a lady, put on a dress, blouse, and cover yourself out of respect for those present.
3. Toothpicks are used in the bathroom. Like brushing, makeup, cleaning your nose, ears and teeth.
4. *The glass is taken by the stem and the little finger should not be lifted when drinking any drink in a glass, glass, or cup.*
5. *Take care of our posture when walking, standing, and sitting. On a sidewalk or sidewalk, the gentleman walks to the side of the street and the lady walks towards the buildings. In a showroom, cinema, or theater to move into your place, do it by watching the stage.*
6. *When sitting and crossing your legs, you should not touch your feet with or without shoes nor is it appropriate to place them on the table; to show the soles... it is not appropriate either.*
7. *In public places, give way or seat to the ladies, as well as the disabled people, the elderly, pregnant women, or someone - whether it be man or woman - who kindly deserves your help.*

Chapter *Five*

♥ Between approach and caresses

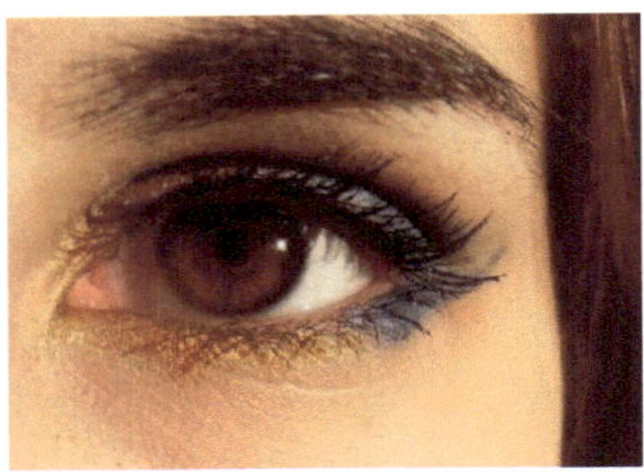

"For a glance, a world; for a smile, a sky; for a kiss... I do not know what I would give you for a kiss!"
Gustavo Adolfo Bécquer.

If you managed to reach this chapter without being involved in caresses or physical contact, I congratulate you! You have managed to give more importance to your neurons, and your intellectual side than to your hormones. That allows you to make better decisions. It is like sitting at a negotiating table after several glasses of wine. This way you will not have the clarity to think fully with your five senses. You will not be ready to decide what trading points favor the company you represent, or you are personally.

Think for a moment about the following questions: Can you imagine a teenage girl having sex and getting pregnant? or the kid who finds out he is going to be a parent when he has not finished developing physically or mentally? If for an adult analyzing all the points exposed in the previous chapters is not easy, for teens it will be even more complicated. That is why I believe that sex education provided by schools and parents should not only teach them how to use contraception but should also emphasize that our body is not an amusement park but a sacred place. It is worth mentioning that before you turn 22, your priority should be your studies. And then prepare yourself financially, as well as mentally. To achieve your true independence as a human being and in turn, be able to provide yourself with a good future.

In the old days, women married at the age of fifteen, and men at the age of twenty and imagine that by the age of forty many had passed away. People were dying noticeably young compared to this time. People now live until the age of eighty, ninety or more. So why rush? The ideal is to accomplish the stages of life, climb the ladder of our existence step by step; because if you do not, you will later see forty-year-olds behaving like teenagers. This is usually because at fifteen they were living as if they were twenty-five years old, and by then they did not live the stages of life that belonged to them.

This is the age where you can date in a group of young people. You can enjoy the beach, practice a sport, visit places where you get carried away by music, by the rhythm. Dancing with different partners without strings attached and without compromises. And especially, without having to be touched disrespectfully by anyone. Only you must be the one who makes the decision of the one who touches your body or not. We know that some people get caught up in very harmful relationships where - in extreme cases - physical or verbal abuse exist. People who feel entangled in a relationship that, more than loving, becomes a relationship based on sex. Then because they do not have the experience of life or because of their immaturity, they do not know how to get out of such cumbersome or compromising situations.

It is also important to mention the level of commitment they can bring to the love relationship. For example, if you have a plate of food in front of you that you do not want to eat, it is not recommended that you take a fork to try and play with the food. In this case it is preferable to let someone else enjoy this dish. It will also happen to someone you are not really interested in. It is better not to get involved if you know it is not for you. And as the saying goes: keep your nose out of it. And if you do not like alcoholic beverages, you should not drink them either. This can also be applied to people. For example, if you have plans to move to London, and are currently living in Mexico City, do not excite a person, and make her or him believe that the relationship has a future, when you already know that it will not have a chance to grow.

Therefore, it is recommended that you be honest. If you are also about to move from the country, you are not going to have a stable relationship with your new acquaintance. Unless you feel like you found your half-orange and this person stirred love at first sight in you. But if this isn't the case, do not fool another human being or play with someone else's feelings, right? It is like I want to plant a tree and I would like you to join me for the rest of my life or at least much of it. I must find the right time. Should it be Spring or Fall, that it receives the necessary amount of water, and that it is also in the right terrain and climate. It also happens with relationships. When we want to get the best out of the relationship, the ideal is to have the right conditions. In other words, "if love were like a tree, the roots would be your own love. The more you love yourself, the more fruits your tree will give to others and the more sustainable it will be over time"- Riso. And Gabriel García

Márquez is not left behind by his beautiful phrase: "I love you, not because of who you are, but for who I am when I am with you." Remember that for the relationship to be beneficial for both of us, it will also depend on us wanting to be better human beings every day.

Until now you feel that your way of acting and talking tells you that you would like to know another type of behavior closer – lovingly speaking – with the person you already shortlisted. You have also already used quality time-related language and enjoy your partner when they share time together. They have applied the saying: "No pain, no gain."

I would like to comment that there are seven virtues and seven sins worth mentioning:

virtues	**sins**
temperance	pride
charity	avarice
diligence	envy
patience	wrath
kindness	lust
humility	gluttony
chastity	sloth

That man or woman who is not diligent and who will have no qualms about having several affairs at once. Keep in mind that this person could be the father or mother of your children. So, ask yourself: Is it worth moving into a more serious relationship with this person or do you run away when you are still on time?

Sayings to keep in mind:

"If you want to know a person, travel with him or her." Or "If you want to know a person, give him or her power."

About giving him power, it can be interpreted as in a job or when receiving a title. For example, give the position or title of boyfriend to a friend. As a friend he was excellent, as a boyfriend, he is jealous, absorbing, rude and/or dominant. It can also be applied to a woman.

Remember that people have qualities and flaws. However, there are some non-serious defects and others that are difficult to bear. Of these fourteen (14) situations, discuss which ones you might live with and which are inadmissible to you:

1. He or she does not behave properly when he or she accompanies you to social events, like using his or her cell phone all the time.

2. His/her table manners are not right. For example: how he/she uses the knife as a dagger and places his/her elbow on the table with the cutlery on the sides of the plate as if they were oars.

3. He touches you in inappropriate parts of your body without your consent and even in public.

4. You have seen him/her acting incorrectly many times even with a spoiled child's "tantrums" if you contradict him/her.

5. Elegance and good taste are not part of his/her personality. His/her favorite outfit is being almost naked. At a formal wedding, she shows up with a miniskirt, or he dresses in a blue shirt and extravagant tie. Photographers try to place them at the ends of photos, so they can be erased.

6. He is a man who does not open a car door or get up when the ladies come to a place. And if he is generally not courteous or attentive - not even with his mother or grandmother - this indicates that less will be so with you. And she lacks kindness.

7. When he opens his mouth, he curses a lot and does not respect the presence of the ladies, or she talks like a person that just got out of jail for men (not even women's) - because of the vocabulary she uses.

So, beware if you find that your partner has any of the first seven defects on this list; some, if they so decide and make the effort of at least... try, can improve their bad behavior over time. There are three proverbs that can guide you in making decisions related to your partner's search. *Correct the wise and make him wiser, correct the fool, and you will make him your enemy*; *He who walks with wolves learns to howl*; and that's why they recommend, birds of each feather flock together, to achieve a better love relationship. Now let us continue with other non-qualities:

1. He is aggressive. And he does not mind ridiculing you in front of his family or your friends.

2. You have seen him/her using drugs.

3. He or she is not generally respectful of anyone.

4. His/her bipolarity is notorious: one day he/she is nice and the next day an ogre.

5. He/she does not respect the 10 commandments of God's law or fulfill the precepts of any belief he/she supposedly professes.

6. If she is a woman, she likes to flirt with everybody. And if he has a man, he is not a monogamist.

7. If a serious problem of any kind arises – it could be a disease – some work situation or serious problems with acquaintances or even strangers, he or she stays out of the way, to the point that he or she disconnects from the situation, leaves the place and/or even ends up blaming you for what happened or the mistakes of others. In other words, you do not feel like you have support or solidarity for yourself.

It should be mentioned that, if your partner possesses any of the last seven defects, living day to day with a person with these characteristics is like being on a roller coaster, where it will be a constant climb, then go down and turn... a super awkward situation. Only if you have a doctorate in how to improve human behavior, have time, and possess the soul of a martyr, maybe with a lot of patience you will succeed in the person's progress in the way he/she acts, and if you can get him/her to improve all his/her flaws, congratulations! You could even be nominated for the Guinness Book Records. Do you know any such cases? Unfortunately, no one can give you a 100% guarantee of a change in behavior. Besides, if he beats you up, you could end up in the hospital. People with these qualities are not the most suitable to form a home or a family.

They should also agree on the issue of finance. In a relationship money is one of the most relevant points to maintain a good relationship. And this must be clear. There is a saying: when hunger walks through the door, love jumps out the window. Therefore, when you are going to make the decision to find your ideal partner, here are the little details to consider. Understand that by ideal it does not mean the perfect relationship, for perfection does not exist, and only God possesses it. The ideal I mean, it is not just that pleasure you feel when you're together, it's also feeling that you really have an ally by your side and that you make a good team in the broad sense of the word.

By far we have noticed the basics of our partner, although sometimes we will not know him fully even if we live for many years with our life partner. A psychologist friend once told me the following: you marry one person and divorce another. When after twenty years of marriage I saw the father of my children in the courthouse, I asked myself where was that wonderful man who wrote me the most beautiful love letters, and with whom I would succeed - that happy, and in love - to marry and have three wonderful and adored children? What I can tell you is that he had everything a woman could hope for. He had physical beauty, was polite, was cultured, professional, and had many other qualities. However, there were two important points that I never noticed: we had no like-minded tastes, and he was a man who, being married, accepted flirting, and something else... of some women. A very accepted pattern of behavior and even celebrated in some cultures, but not by me. While engaged, one of the important points we both agreed on was that a third person was not welcome in our relationship. Unfortunately, he forgot that previous covenant between the two.

These situations got us to sign our separation after two decades of marriage. Even though I got divorced, I do not recommend you marry the idea that if things do not work out, you will get divorced. It would be like investing in a company - which you consider successful at first - with the idea of failing. When you start a project, you start with all the energy and desire to be successful. Not the other way around. If the worst happens, you get up again and prepare better. Whether it is the discouragement of unrequited love, a company that failed, or simply the next challenge with which life surprises you.

Always remember that no matter how annoying they are, you should not lose control over yourself. Since screaming, and ill-treatment never benefit anyone. I can mention that the ones that are most affected by a couple's disagreements are children. Therefore, if we want successful adults, family members, good professionals, and socially with their stable lives, we must set a good example for them. And even though there is marital separation, parents must ensure that the rupture harms their children as little as possible. You must not speak ill of your ex-partner. In my case, and more, if the person who asks me what happened to my first husband, does it in front of my children, I always answer, "We are not compatible." The other details are not necessary.

It would be difficult for young people who had a childhood and/or adolescence affected by their parents' relationship, to consider this failure and avoid the same mistakes they made.

I would like to share this beautiful message with you:

A Tibetan story tells that one day an old sage asked his followers the following: – *Why do people yell when they are angry?*

The men thought for a few moments:

"Because we lose our cool," said one, "that's why we scream.

-But why scream when the other person is next to you? The sage asked, is it not possible to speak to him in a low voice? Why are you yelling at a person?

The sage continued:

– What happens when two people fall in love? They do not yell at each other, but they talk softly; why? Because their hearts are so close. The distance between them is exceedingly small.

The sage smiled and said:

– When they fall even more in love, what happens? They do not talk, they just whisper, and they become even closer in their love.

Remember, our mind is immensely powerful. Let us always look at life with optimism, not as if we were walking with a gray cloud over us. Thinking that if lightning strikes, it is going to fall on us. To think positively, to prepare ourselves, and to accomplish it. Make plans to go and see a beautiful and romantic city like Paris - if you do not already know it.

At this point in the relationship and after several outings to different places and going through different circumstances, you would already like to have a real romantic night where you can let your guard down because the other person inspires confidence. If at the end of the date, between the looks and the previous signs, you notice that your companion begins to approach his face towards yours to give you a kiss... that marks the perfect end to it.

Chances are you are going to enjoy it because the paved ground already has better conditions in that love relationship, and both feel the kiss in a compatible way. Instead, if we precipitate that kiss on our first outing there is the possibility that our partner will take it as something unpleasant and even as an invasion of their private space.

Who are the best kissers according to the zodiac? Mundo Actualidad in its publication of January 22, 2018 commented that a kiss can be memorable. But that it will depend on the chemistry between the two people, the type of kiss and even some magic with the other person. According to Rutgers

University, the perfect kiss should be wet and with the mouth wide open by women. I would also like to share with you the way of kissing each star sign:

Aries. *– Give tender and passionate kisses. They do not usually ask permission to give you a kiss, and you are taken by surprise.*

Taurus. *- Lovers of long and deep kisses. She loves that while kissing her partner, she touches his hair and gets carried away.*

Gemini. *- Deliver kisses of all kinds. Your kissing is not defined as it depends on your mood.*

Cancer. *- They are very safe when giving a kiss. They are crazy to be spoken to in every kiss through whispers.*

Leo. *- When you do not love your kisses are cold and shy. Conversely, when you are truly in love you are completely in love.*

Virgo. *- It is the sign that gives meticulous and detailed kisses. Your kissing may change as your partner emotionally connects with him/her.*

Libra. *- Excellent kissers. They are characterized by giving enveloping kisses and walking the body of the other person with their lips.*

Scorpio. *- Intense to give kisses. They arouse strong emotions in their partners.*

Sagittarius. *- Tend to give seductive and slow kisses until you reach hot and creative kisses that drive your partner crazy.*

Capricorn. *- Give shy kisses, however, when you are confident you recognize what your partner wants. He is a conqueror and could know the desires of his loved one.*

Aquarium. *- Deliver creative kisses that can be warm and distant. Violent or delicate and provocative.*

Pisces. *- Sensitive and dreamy, and your kisses go in the same line.*

As we can see, there is an interesting variety of kisses. In addition, even if we are experts in giving an excellent French kiss, this does not mean that they should practice it with everyone, nor that they should demonstrate this skill at every opportunity. That is why it is important that everything arrives in due time.

How did you feel about that first kiss? Was it sexy? At first the ideal is the rubbing of the lips and gradually his lips will open to cross his tongue with yours. You felt the best thing your whole body was showing that you were in tune with that long-awaited moment. Maybe you come home like you were floating on air, or it might be that – chemically speaking – you do not see a future for this love relationship.

It is good to mention that every showing of love is a private matter. The kisses, caresses and even those words that some lovers use privately are not well seen in front of other people. Example: "My honey filled sweetheart, sugar cube and some other cloying expressions." Maybe you smiled reading the example or even blushed; that is how a lot of people feel when you hear a lover using those kinds of expressions in public. In private, it unleashes your displays of love and romantic expressions, but in public – including social media – take care of your loving behavior out of respect for the people around you. By now you will know what kind of relationship you are going to have. It may be that they are already dating with a view to getting to know each other better and then taking the step to commitment, and then... marriage. There are cases where a child posts on his/her profile on Facebook, to be in a relationship and his "alleged lover" posts on his profile, single and only needs to add... uncommitted and available. If you both are happy with the relationship you lead and agree; no problem, it is the decision of both. The problem exists when men and women are on different frequencies. Or one of us is not being given the right place by the partner.

Is this couple on the same frequency?

Important Etiquette Points Between Approaches and Caresses...

1. *Love demonstrations in public are not appropriate. It is OK to be seen holding hands, a hug, a cross of glances, a kiss on the cheek, forehead... even in the hand. And in the mouth? In private. In public a kiss on the mouth is only well seen on your wedding day unless it is so discreet that it does not bother the people present.*
2. *You must keep your word.*
3. *To be sincere is not the same as being rude.*
4. *It is especially important to dress according to the occasion.*
5. *Gentlemen will wear long-sleeved, white shirts when attending formal events.*
6. *Women should not make an excessive use of accessories.*
7. *As serious as the situation is, remember that people understand each other by talking. When you are upset you should control the situation and never verbally assault the other person with negative qualifiers or loud words, let alone physically attack them. "Do not lay a finger on a woman." Nor should a woman hit a man.*

Chapter *Six*

♥ What We Had Been Waiting for

"The sexual act without love never bridges the gap between two human beings, except momentarily..."
Erich Fromm

The expected moment arrived because we have already passed the tests of the previous chapters, and decided to arrange an appointment in a romantic place. If you are very conservative you will think about having sex after you are married by the Church - synagogue, temple, or court - and a priest, rabbi, pastor, or judge gives you the blessing and/or declares you husband and wife. However, if the decision to have your first romantic night is without the legality of marriage, you can have a loving encounter in a special place prepared for the occasion. In your apartment or your partner's apartment... maybe in a hotel. From there – for a large part – will derive the magic of a love encounter. At this time more than in any other situation, we will be able to demonstrate our politeness with our lady or our gentleman.

There are hotels that have gained international fame where couples can spend an unforgettable honeymoon. They have beautiful views, Jacuzzis, Turkish baths, or small pools within the spacious and wonderfully comfortable rooms. These can be very modern or go back to the era of European romanticism. It will all depend on your tastes and the decision you make with your partner. It can be on a mountain with a lit fireplace in the room. In the middle of a safari, in the romantic city par excellence –Paris, or another famous city – or near the coast, if you like the beach. Usually the favorite destination of many couples is related to a fabulous sea view. Whether on dry land or on an island. The Pacific or Caribbean islands are highly sought after for this type of occasion.

Take care of the little details at that special time. Like a bottle of champagne with its flute glasses or some exquisite non-alcoholic drink, some floral arrangement, sheets that are made with good cotton or linen -if the weather is warm. The important thing is that both agree with the chosen location. Complement this wonderful moment with candles, pleasant music, and absolute exclusivity for your partner in this time and space, designed just for you. You can condition the place with a rich aroma that stimulates sexual desire, such as the smell of cinnamon, jasmine, ginger, lavender, rose, sandalwood, or vanilla.

It is advisable to have a glass of water or another drink nearby. Cotton or disposable hand towels are also useful on both night tables whether it is a hotel or a bedroom. If it is another kind of venue, look for the place that is comfortable for you to keep at hand the things that are required for such a special time. The important thing is that after the magical moment, each one does not need to run to the bathroom to clean up properly, but that pleasantly, you can remain embraced enjoying the company of your beloved after such special self-giving. So, it will be more pleasant for you to remember this wonderful love encounter.

In other words, what can I recommend before, during, and after making love?

- Maintain good education always and above all at such a special time as this.
- Be cautious and consider adequate protection to prevent pregnancy.
- Use your imagination.
- Body and oral hygiene.
- Wear a sexy, and elegant outfit to sleep.
- It will be more interesting if you gradually undress, or undress each other, than to present yourself completely naked.
- Take off our stockings and socks.
- Be patient and enjoy the preamble to the sexual encounter with passionately sweet kisses, and gentle caresses in your erogenous zones.
- Be empathetic. Think not only of our satisfaction but also of our partner's.
- Use flattering words, especially the gentleman.
- Communicate to the partner how we feel. We must not be mute.
- Do not force your partner into situations that are not pleasant for him/her.
- At the end of the coitus, you should use the cotton or disposable towels that I mentioned before, to avoid keeping our intimate areas moist, and thus get rid of bacteria.
- Drink water or any other liquid you want, if deemed necessary.

- It is good to prevent -in addition to pregnancy- possible infections.

There are couples who romantically take a shower together. Others prefer after this beautiful moment, to simply rest embraced feeling their hearts satisfied as well as their bodies. Also, it is advisable not to wear the same underwear that we had before the loving approach.

Now let us visualize this beautiful and long-awaited encounter. They arrive at the place where everything has a special magic. The animal instinct that prevails more in man than in woman, as the gentleman that he is, he keeps under control. And thinking as an empathetic person, he considers the feelings of the lady, so that the lady does not feel at any time sexually used. Then each one flows as they feel comfortable, they slowly undress under a dim electric light or with candles. Perhaps a gentleman's massage to the lady, his kisses and caresses, will make her become so relaxed that she feels that her body is floating in the air, and that all those prejudices, and myths- more if this is her first time- are numbed in her mind to allow herself to enjoy these loving-sexual manifestations. The gentleman in turn can culminate his long-awaited sexual moment with the beautiful damsel. Who has accompanied him even with sweet caresses in his most intimate parts, which will help him to feel completely satisfied and wrapped in the most desired love. They will have lived an incredibly special moment for their lives, which they can always remember in the mental album of their experiences whenever they wish. The other details, I leave them to your imagination.

Since I was noticeably young, I heard that a gentleman never talks about a lady. I think it means that what happens within a loving relationship will only be between them and no one else. Even less, spreading out what happened inside a room where a couple had a beautiful love-filled sexual experience. That pleasant and intimate moment is to be enjoyed and remembered by them - just by them. It is not for it to appear in newspapers or social media, let alone to be boasted with family and/or friends. What if it did not all turn out to be fireworks at the first time? I suggest you give yourself another chance and as many as necessary, if you feel the relationship is worth it.

There are cases of couples who, although everything seemed to strengthen gradually, ultimately did not turn out, as in some personal examples of friends I know. And that even though they were already adults, and could analyze these kinds of situations, they were disappointed because they simply lacked some important ingredient for them. And those encounters also culminated unsuccessfully. For example, in the first case I want to share with you, they were both extremely interested since they met. They were quite excited and took a nice vacation in Cancun. Upon returning from the trip they decided to separate as they concluded that, unfortunately, they were not sexually compatible. In the second case, they did not have to go that far. They chose a beautiful boutique hotel in the same city where they lived. Those hotels that highlight the symbol of the pineapple, which represents the exotic, welcome and hospitality. After a romantic dinner, toasting with a bottle of champagne and having consummated the sexual act, not only was there no sparks of colors or supreme emotions in the room - on the contrary - for my friend it was a total disenchantment!

On the other hand, let us remember that at the end of a couple's relationship, we must say goodbye elegantly. We can understand that a bond is over, and we must always consider the feelings of the people involved in this relationship. Always practicing empathy. Remember that you should never do to another person, that which you would not want to be done to you.

Continuing with the hypothesis that the relationship works, I suggest that from the first time you have a loving encounter where you share your apartment, you take care of the details. The bed, bathroom, and other places of the venue where you will meet, as well as your behavior. Remember that as I mentioned earlier, the lady and the gentleman are known at the table and in a game. In addition, I would add that the lady and the gentleman are known at the table, in the game, in the bathroom and... in intimacy too. Ladies and gentlemen do not leave everything messy wherever you go. Close the cap of the toothpaste, shampoo, rinse, or liquid soap. Brush your teeth in a way that does not splash the mirror in which you are being reflected. Do not leave the towel out of place or in the middle of the bathroom. Unless they are in a hotel, and so tell the maid or room service that towels need to be replaced with clean ones. Put the papers and trash in the trash. Do not leave the bar of soap full of hair or other particles like beach sand. If there is a curtain in the shower, please close it so that the water does not leak out. Have a towel on hand to dry before leaving the shower area. This way, you will avoid wetting the bathroom floor unnecessarily. Remember that the bathroom or vanity is ideal for grooming your ears, nose or cutting your nails or combing both your hair, and so that the ladies can do their makeup comfortably. If you feel any flatulence, this is also the right place for it. In such circumstances, do not forget the aromatic candle or light a match to minimize the uncomfortable smell.

You should have learned these details at your parents' house. But if you missed the day, they were explaining them to your brothers, it is good to learn about them, and put them into practice.

Many of us were clueless about many facts, essentially love and sexual relationships when we were in pre-teens, we repeated jokes that we listened to adults, and we did not know the true meaning of what we were saying. A dear friend listening to one of these jokes believed that if a girl were kissed, she would become pregnant. We were thirteen years old and we still played with dolls. Some thirteen current years are entertained with dolls, but of flesh and blood kind. And the saddest thing is that sometimes wanting to play the game of love, they get pregnant. That is why I see with concern how some young people begin to practice their sexual relations very soon, being carried away by peer pressure, and without making a good inquiry. Excellent theme for a book.

Some women came to their marriage with only the information given to them by some people close to them, such as some family members and friends. There were also girlfriends looking for more testimonies, and experiences in books and love films about the famous first night of the love meeting.

In the naivety of my time, I tell you that complicated situations also occurred because we did not really know who we were marrying. For example, I met a case of a newlywed who spent her honeymoon traveling, eating exquisitely, visiting museums where she could see men's naked bodies in artwork, but she never saw her husband's during that trip. So back home she remained a virgin and out of embarrassment, she dared not tell anyone. Six months into marriage, her husband confesses that he is attracted to men and not women. Unfortunately, this man married because of social pressure and not of his own free will. This issue – in the past – was taboo and this man was socially vetoed. Although homosexuality is not one hundred percent well seen, and there are places in the world where it is punished; today, in most nations there is more openness in relation to this issue, and it is no longer just mentioned in movies, TV shows or books; but there are also countries where same-sex marriage is legally allowed. Ideally, in these cases, these people feel family and community support to be accepted as homosexuals, although the situation is not expected by society or by many religions, you cannot hide reality and pretend to be heterosexual, when The person is not. Unfortunately, because situations like these can harm other human beings – such as – the girl I tell you about in the story, who had a hard time recovering from this deception.

For this and other reasons, there are parents who, although quite conservative, allow their children to experience an intimate encounter or to go on holiday with their fiancé before they get married.

I would like to tell you something especially important. If you notice strange or abnormal behavior even if you are inexperienced on the intimate-sexual subject, or have gone untouched to the encounter, always consult with a close family member or a professional in the field. Because no matter how in love and polite we are - if we have doubts - it is better to inform ourselves properly. Likewise, there are also cases in which we might feel aggression from our sexual partner and this behavior we should never be accepted. Under no circumstances can we allow another human being to harm us. The normality or abnormality of a relationship will be noticed whether both are happy with the practice of a method or not.

I also suggest that because some young couples today have decided to live together, I do not recommend that they stay in this kind of free union. If you already know that you love and get along, feel very engaged and are prepared financially and professionally, it would be good for you to formalize your relationship. Whether we like it or not, say that we do not like the little paper, it talks and matters. Also, when you live with someone, it is like when you rent a place, and when you get married it is like when you buy a home. The person pays more attention and strives more to take care of his house when it is bought than when it is rented, do not you think? This does not mean that our partner is our property and belongs to us. It means we are committed to make sure our relationship works.

Anecdote. - *The case of a couple - a Swiss and his Italian lover - decided to move together to Japan, where he had an excellent job at a multinational company. After ten years of cohabitation, the lover dies and all the belongings that existed inside the house are inherited by his wife, since he never divorced. The property was in someone else's name. This person had no scruples and took ownership on the grounds that his deal was with the Swiss man and not with*

the Italian woman. The multinational company where the lover worked had no way of protecting her, as they were not legally married. And the Italian woman, overnight, after giving herself up body and soul to this Swiss executive, was left with nothing. She had to leave Tokyo - where they resided - empty-handed and heartbroken. And thus, had to go to start a new life in her home country -Italy. Therefore, it is advisable to do things properly.

Now, you have reviewed a lot of points about your partner. You have gone to see the rings and you will even be reading a book about wedding protocol.

Here are some of the most relevant items to consider:

- Have the right amount of time to start with the preparations.
- The place where marriage will be officiated.
- The place for the celebration.
- The wedding-party.
- How many people you want to invite and who.
- What kind of dress code you are going to select.
- Choose the type of food and drinks.
- The cake.
- Desserts.
- The décor.
- Hire the photographer.
- The person who will make the video for you.
- The music to be played at the wedding party.
- The schedules to coordinate every stage of that day.

Extra details, such as the "Traditional Crazy Hour" if there is going to be a dance at the party, which consists of a moment where guests dance wearing masks and colorful ornaments.

When the couple already arrives at this moment, it must be so coordinated, that decision-making on each of the points mentioned will be a pleasant moment.

Let us look at the situations before. When my sisters, cousins and I got married, the parents were the ones who made almost all the decisions on the points mentioned above, even deciding who the wedding guests would be. It was assumed that it was a presentation of the young couple to the social circle to which their parents belonged. We could select our closest friends, even if it were a wedding of 900 guests – as was the wedding of my younger sister, or 200 guests as mine was with the father of my children. It was not appropriate to ask the guests for anything and much less for money, although close family and friends did prefer to give an envelope with a card and gift money to the newly married couple. Especially when they planned to live abroad. The gifts were chosen – as now – in specialized stores for weddings and if anyone asked, we could comment on a registry. Nowadays, some couples do not allow suggestions from their parents and there are young people who choose everything and even pay for their weddings without any help from their parents. And as the saying goes: "*who pays, commands*".

The day you get married you will hear many of your family and family friends remind you of popular sayings or give you incredibly wise advice. Listen to them! Since with age comes wisdom. Here are a few:

- Do not use double standards.

- Please your wife, treat her like a queen, so she will raise your children as princes.
- No one should come between husband and wife.
- Your son is as you raise him, your husband is as you accustom him.
- Do not go to sleep upset with your wife/husband.
- *When you socialize, join the group. Do not hold hands isolated in a corner of the event. It is better to stay home than to behave like this in a social meeting or party.*
- *Sleep is sacred. Respect each other's sleep when you have vacation days or weekends, and do not have to work.*
- *Peter's wife must not only be, but also appear to be.* It also applies to men, we must be consistent with our feelings, thoughts, and our actions. If I love my girlfriend or wife, I must not disrespect her by having affairs with other women.

I remember before my eldest daughter got married, we sat down and I told her, "Always remember that you come from a family of honorable women. Your great-great-grandmother was an honorable woman like your great-grandmother, your grandmother, and your mother. You must always be an excellent wife faithful to your husband. Do not do it for him, do it for you. Always take care of your good reputation." Likewise, I think that not only women should be faithful to their husbands. Men must also respect his marriage.

Both must always keep in mind their marriage vows:

"I, – the name of the bride – love you as a wife and I give myself to you. I promise to be faithful to you in joy and sorrow. In sickness and in health. Wealth and poverty. Until death do us part."

"I, – the groom's name – love you as a husband and I give myself to you. I promise to be faithful to you in joy and sorrow. In sickness and in health. Wealth and poverty. Until death do us part."

It is hard, when life confronts us with divorce after many years of marriage, and we look back at the day we made our vows. Sometimes, year after year we try to have a good relationship with our partner, but there are cases where a separation is healthier for the spouses, and their children than staying married. Although it may seem like a lie, children sense everything and, while they will miss not having their parents together, they will benefit if they do not feel in the middle of a relationship where love is over. He is lost her respect or vice versa. There is no good communication. It is no longer important to share moments as a couple. Tried couples' therapy and it did not work. There are no goals together. Among many other reasons.

Once a dear friend told me this: I plan to divorce, but I am not sure what it will be like. To which I said: the answer you are going to give yourself, can you imagine being old by his side? Her answer was no. Later she made the decision of ending her marriage relationship. Today, she has developed very well at the professional level and her son, already a man, thanked his mother for the decision. Because having been two unhappy people together, today they are a man and a woman who have achieved much apart from each other. Their faces reflect the peace and happiness they would not have been able to achieve if they remained married today. In this case – the divorce – was a good decision.

There are questions that help us know if we want to continue in the benefit of our union. That is why I asked my friend this question, can you imagine yourself with your husband when you are old? There are times when there are conditions for a couple's relationship to work. Where, despite the highs and lows this loving relationship may have, there is such a sincere solidity and feelings that it deserves our energy to continue together. Instead, in other relationships, whatever is done is done, only the waste of time and energy is achieved, fighting to save the insurmountable.

As an example, my parents were married for more than half a century. Even if we rated them from one to one hundred, they would not have scored the 100 points. But what I learned from them, and that helped me a lot by establishing a marriage and raising my children, was this:

- They liked to feed their love relationship, going out together, trips, phone calls at opportune times and with other details.
- They listened to each other.
- My father always pleased my mother and vice versa.
- My father believed a lot in the sixth sense of his wife. My mother always believed in my father's good judgment.
- They gave each other their place in front of us and with other people.

- Care for each other was especially important. They took care of each other when they got sick.
- Their bed was always clean and tidy. They never slept in street clothes on their bed, even if they went to sleep their usual nap.
- They gave great importance to eating together as a family.
- The table talk at home was very entertaining.
- Their discussions were in private.
- They both agreed when we asked for permission to go out.
- They accompanied each other to their social gatherings.
- They went around the world holding hands.
- They supported and complemented each other very well. My mother never cooked, and my father made excellent dishes. To my liking, the most exquisite and simple turkey was prepared by my father. If you want the recipe, I can give it to you by email or privately on one of my social networks.
- They stuck to their promise in the good and the bad.
- They slept hugging each other until the day my father passed away.

There will be times when you will ask yourself: Does the person I am dating have a future in my life? Is it worth the time I am spending? Does he value me? And there will be other questions that you will discover over the course of your relationship.

To leave a smile on your lips, I share the following joke:

A couple of very innocent and inexperienced peasants get married and after the party they head to the hotel room.

The new husband asks the new wife, "Do you want to undress or what?"

She shyly replies: "Well, we undress." And she is embarrassed but starts undressing.

So, he asks another question: "Do you want us to take a bath or what?"

She replies, "Well, we bathe." And he is heading for the shower.

Already cleansed they get inside the sheets: and he asks another question again: "Do you want to sleep or what?"

She, all blushing, says, "Well, first whatever and then we fall asleep."

Very decisive, the newlywed, isn't she? I hope that, in your case, maybe you have not married yet because you prefer to read the next chapter of this book, before making the decision to:

- Give the engagement ring to your girlfriend.
- If you are the girl, give a resounding yes, when your boyfriend proposes to you.

- If you are an unconventional couple and it is the woman who is preparing to ask the groom's hand and wants to be sure of his decision.

Or as if it were a multiple-choice exam...

- None of the above, but I want to read the book to the end.

Important Etiquette Points of what we look forward to...

1. Hygiene care is super important.
2. When you need to use the bathroom, it is not correct to mention the situation. It is better to excuse yourself discreetly.
3. Leave the bathroom tidy and lower the toilet lid.
4. The information of another person's cell phone is not reviewed, or the correspondence of another person is *not to be opened*, nor is the wallet *or purse* without the owner's permission.
5. *You do not write publicly what not everyone should read. Take care of your privacy.*
6. Do not abuse anyone and less of our loved ones.
7. *Do not end a family, work, friendly; and even less, a romantic relationship, through social networks. It is done in person.*

Chapter *Seven*

♥ The importance of your partner's full knowledge

"It is not the appearance; it is the essence.
It is not the money; it is the good education.
It is not the clothes; it is the class." Coco Chanel

As this book puts it, the couple I am talking about is the one we want to have for life and not for a simple night of crazy adventure. As a result, I will give you valuable tools and information for both men and women. For everyone, the feeling of security is pleasant. However, when we seek this protection, we must be sure that they are really protecting us. Without feeling limited, used, controlled, or minimized. On the contrary, where we feel complemented and accompanied with each other in the pleasant moments, and in the not so pleasant moments of our day to day. For example, as with the simple gesture when we sit down to enjoy our food or to solve some inconvenience that arises, such as if your puppy is missing, and you go out together in search of the pet. That is why I have insisted from the beginning the importance of always doing things right.

I know that sexuality is especially important in a relationship; however, there are also many other points that we must consider if we want to have a good bond with our partner. I believe that the most accurate way to fall completely in love is when these three elements are involved: the mind, the soul, and the heart. It is the heart that binds us to this person in such a wonderful way that we feel pleased, happy, and complete with his company. So, while the soul feels our affinity, our brain must also be considered. For while the heart is fluttering in the clouds, the mind makes us visualize the reality that the heart does not see. The images of the happy couple who have formed a true stable couple have taken their time, so that we can make a much broader list than I mentioned in the first chapters. In these lists the positive things that they both like should predominate more than those details that tarnish the relationship with negativity. They would not make it overnight.

There are also cases of couples who started in an extraordinary way where a promising future was envisioned. However, after going on to their lives together, they noticed that it was time to discuss some elements of the relationship. It is important that the list of things you like is longer than the list of things you dislike. And this is where a good time is presented to reflect. And even more so when they have not taken the step of living together, committing, or getting married.

In the previous chapters, we discussed several of the situations that it would be advisable to consider in a couples' relationship. We can compare the situation as if you had been driving a car on a road of dangerous curves, in which case you must be alert and with your five senses on the steering wheel. Having considered the alerts regarding the couples' relationship from the previous chapters; from now on, it is like you are driving on an easier road.

I share with you these wise words which for some of you will serve as a reflection and for others as confirmation.

Venezuelan writer Arturo Uslar-Pietri expressed in one of his television shows his vision of how he defined a couple. Uslar-Pietri, commented that man and woman were not equal beings. He said, "they are different and complement each other." He mentioned that it was particularly important to learn to relate properly and that they had to take the time to get to know each other well. He also mentioned that many couples focused mostly on the sexual part of their relationship, not realizing that the time they spend together in passionate moments is small proportionally to what they will spend sharing other activities.

It could add these seven (7) Cs. Based on my book "Living in Harmony". They will help you have a good relationship:

- ♥ **Cherishing and Love**
- ♥ **Courtesy**
- ♥ **Communication**
- ♥ **Cooperation or collaboration**
- ♥ **Comprehension**
- ♥ **Consideration**
- ♥ **Commitment**

♥ **Cherishing and love** are to show love for our partner in everything we do for that person. "For the one who loves, a thousand objections do not come to form a doubt; for the one who does not love, a thousand proofs do not become a certainty." Anonymous.

♥ **Courtesy** when living with an educated and classy person, will make the relationship more pleasant. To complement this idea, a courteous person is educated and keeps the rules of courtesy. Education does not fight anyone. That is why if you choose the lover who owns it, at critical moments in your relationship, it will be essential to help you get out of the crisis.

♥ **Communication** is learning -in addition to speaking- listening to your husband or partner.

♥ **Cooperation or collaboration** is to understand that currently both must work not only outside the house, but also within your home.

♥ **Comprehension** is understanding your partner. Also, trying to alleviate your partner's distress.

♥ **Consideration** is respect, understanding and being kind to our partner. Be empathetic and place yourself in the place of the loved one.

♥ **Commitment** is to keep our word, especially the one we gave in the vows when we married. "I, ______, take you, ______, to be my (husband/wife). I promise to be true to you in good times and in bad. I will love you and honor you all the days of my life."

In addition, it would be selfish of us to pretend that our partner's life only revolves around us and that we have no greater contact with family, friends and even classmates or coworkers. Unfortunately, there are human beings who do not realize the importance of maintaining a good relationship with each of our loved ones. The relationships between parents-children, grandparents-grandchildren, brothers, friends, and others, each is irreplaceable by another. No matter how good our life with our partner is, be sure to give each of your loved ones, the right place in your life.

It is also necessary to consider the tasks of the home. For example, if you marry the son of the Perfect Housewife, he will keep in mind that everything related to the house is not his obligation, and that the one who should occupy that position in his home is you, since he does not want to get involved with household chores, because his father didn't either.

Now, this will be a decision you will have to make together. And if you both accept it that way, there will not be a problem. However, if you are a professional woman, and want to develop your career, it will be difficult to take care of your work and all the home chores such as: cooking, washing dishes and clothes, ironing, cleaning, arranging the rooms, dusting, the kitchen, the living room, the bathrooms, sweeping, mopping, polishing wood and silver, removing the cobwebs, changing sheets and towels periodically and also, taking out the trash. This is not to mention the unforeseen events that may occur in a home. In addition, you will have to take care of the extra errands outside the house such as: going to the bank, making the weekly shopping, payments - among many other things. Repair what is damaged and sew the clothes when it is needed. To tend to family and social relationships. Going out to buy the gifts according to the different invitations you receive. And when you thought you had your life under control, kids show up with a whole new list of chores included.

Sounds like a lot of work, doesn't it? That is right, if the person who performs all these functions, does so without help or collaboration of any kind. That is why it is important that when both work outside the house they also share and divide household chores. Here I could mention what we know as acts of service shared with the being you love. Unless – of course – they can afford one or more domestic servants to perform all these tasks, and thus make their lives easier for them. It should be allusion that there are still many girls who do not intend to work away from home because in their family, and in the environment where they operate, the man is the family provider. It is particularly important to take all these points into account in a couple.

There are men who in divorce indicate the fact that only they contribute financially to the home, without valuing all the functions that the wife performs for her husband and children. Many wives spend many hours of the seven days of the week, three hundred and sixty-five days of the year, sometimes without vacation, looking after the welfare of the family. In addition, thanks to them their husbands enjoy excellent business and social relations, which are especially important factors. As my mother says, "In many situations, relationships are more important than money." Many husbands give them the real importance they have in a family, homework, and social relationships. There are cases, where it is the man who works at home while the woman is the one who, through her work, covers the budget, other expenses and savings related to the family. Thank goodness! There are more and more countries, where people who oversee family operation are protected by law.

Anecdote

At a social meeting held in one of the beautiful cities of Latin America, one of the guests told us that - on an occasion - her husband had behaved very distantly with her. When he arrived at his house at dusk, he found her dressed in black. He thought it was strange, but he did not comment. At breakfast he saw her in black again and that night again, her dress was black.

At that moment he realized that something was going on and dared to ask her, "My love, did someone die?"

She replied with a profoundly serious face, "Yes, our great love. That is why I am in mourning."

You can imagine the look on the face of this gentleman who was very much in love with his wife. After the unexpected moment for him, he went out to find a beautiful bouquet of red flowers and took the opportunity to hire some mariachis. After several songs and handing over the flowers, they fired the musicians and calmly cleared up the misunderstanding. In this way, they understood that assumptions can confuse them.

It is always good to ask first before jumping to conclusions. Since then, they have done so to avoid any misunderstanding.

As we have already mentioned before, there are different ways to express our feelings. Gary Chapman's "Five Languages of Love" is immensely helpful in aiding us to have a good relationship with our partner and show our love. I really liked the summary about these five Instagram languages of Integrating the Being. @Integrandoelser in its 2019 publication defines them as follows:

- *Words of Affirmation - This language is about when we express love with words and feel loved through what we hear. When we receive flattery, letters, or declarations of love. Those words that affirm the pride and happiness of being with that person and the positive appreciation you make of him/her. It is that power that we have with the use of words that makes us create a new world to give and receive love.*

- *Acts of Service - It is when we do something like prepare food, have details with each other, take care of each other when we get sick, take care of the home, etc. That is, they are simple acts that demonstrate the interest and love for the other person.*

- *Physical contact - It is the simplest language because words are not needed. It is about giving and receiving hugs, caresses, kissing when saying goodbye and before going to sleep, walking holding hands, etc. It is the first we learn as children because it offers us relief, safety, and affection. It is immensely powerful as physical contact puts our immune system into action to fight diseases.*
- *Receive gifts – In this language we enjoy love giving and/or receiving gifts representing how important we are to each other. It is a detail that is offered in many ways. The important thing is that it is given for the pleasure of sharing or pleasing your loved one and not to achieve a goal.*
- *Quality time - This language is the simple fact of spending time alone -without interruptions - creating the time and space to deepen the relation. Sometimes we neglect these moments that keep our relationship alive. Because remember, love is expressed by sharing moments where our presence is meaningful.*

Now being at this stage where either you decided to share your lives without legal or religious commitment; or either formalizing your relationship into "Mr. and Mrs.", I suggest that of all the plants that periodically must be watered in the home, love should be the priority. So that when your family begins to grow, these children will arrive at a place where respect and good behavior will always be a good example to follow.

On one occasion I heard an older gentleman say, "So why buy the cow if the milk is free." In other words, they discriminated against girls who had pre-marital sex. In addition, it was generally rare for brides to mention to their boyfriends the subject of the ring. And even in the 21st century, it is expected that it will be the gentleman who makes the marriage proposal. There are also cases where the woman is the one who hints at the idea of marriage and most men flee quickly, disappearing never to be seen again. Which has an incredibly positive point, as you will not keep wasting your time with that person who obviously does not merit you, consuming your precious time, and the opportunity to meet someone who would really value you.

Anecdote

I would like to mention that there are women for whom it has worked not only to ask for the ring, but to be the ones who propose marriage to their boyfriends. Today I hear more often, about numerous cases where it is the woman who courageously proposes marriage and the man happily accepts. I heard the first case - of this kind - 18 years ago. He was an American and she was a beautiful and intelligent German lady who, after dating for some time, decided to invite this gentleman to her home country. After noticing that he was accepted by her family and friends, she asks him to marry her. *Upon his return from the invitation to Germany, this somewhat bewildered American came home for dinner alone. He took his time to tell us about the proposal and told us that he had not yet given his answer.*

My husband and I asked him the following three questions:

1. *Do you love her?*
2. *Did you like her family?*
3. *Did you like her country and culture?*

His three answers were: Yes! Yes! Yes!

Today, they remain in a stable marriage and are still happily in love. To complete their happiness, God blessed them with the great joy of having two beautiful children.

According to some religions, we were created in the image and likeness of God and with free will. That is, if God gives us the freedom to make each of our decisions, let us make use of this freedom. That said, having the empathy to think that if the bride (we are going to think it has the boyfriend who takes the initiative), is already waiting to be engaged, he is going to please her. To then take the step, towards that longed-for moment that most couples in love dream of living and experiencing with the loved one. To be able for their friends and family, to recognize the commitment to love each other, to respect each other, to accompany each other in good and bad, until death does them part. And in the presence of the guests, a cameraman(s) and a photographer(s) focused on them, they kiss – that kiss that is socially allowed – amid applause, laughter, and tears of happiness. The music – which they chose together – creates an atmosphere of harmony, when they hold hands and become husband and wife, they pass with their faces radiant with happiness, in front of all the guests.

Every moment is unique and worth living. When we go through difficult situations, remember your wedding day. It will remind you that it is worth to not give up and always continue forward.

In addition to my parents, there are several couples from my family and friends who have already completed Silver Weddings, Golden Weddings and I know one who have already fulfilled their Platinum Weddings. We could also mention several monarchs, great personalities from the world of politics and even show business, which is celebrated by divorces, because of how complicated it is to maintain loving relationships because of the work. This shows that there are marriages that survive their tempests and remain united. I would like to mention a couple who have served more than four decades together, that of Michael Caine and his wife Shakira Baksh.

You can consider that you maintain a good relationship with your partner if you:

♥ Focus on the positive.

♥ Be tolerant of differences.

♥ Try getting out of the routine whenever you can.

♥ Learn to share your bed, belongings, and space in general.

♥ Find a way to improve each day for family well-being.

♥ Give yourselves a passionate kiss daily. That generates oxytocin.

♥ Forgive your partner, and he or she corrects the inappropriate behavior.

♥ Always keep in mind that respect is especially important in human relationships, especially with our partner.

♥ Be faithful sentimentally. This point is particularly important, that is why we repeat it.

♥ Spend the right time and always take care of the details.

♥ When there are difficulties in certain circumstances of their relationship, remember that when there are hurricane-strong winds, palm trees receive less damage during the storm than rigid trees because of their flexibility.

♥ There is a beautiful phrase by the grandfather of a dear friend

- Dr. Jasmin Sánchez - Analyst and Conflict Resolutionist that says: "If you observe something in your wake that makes you uncomfortable and do nothing to fix it, you immediately become complicit in the wrong."

♥ Remember that, if you did not start as friends, with the relationship, your partner should be your best friend, husband, lover, ally, your best fan, and your most trusted person.

Fall in love constantly with the same person, your husband. Have lots of honeymoons, remembering when you were newlyweds.

I tell you; all these points are part of the triumph of many marriages that have been blessed by many years of union. Hopefully, you get the partner you are looking for and adapts to your measurements. If you already have it, I hope that, with the reading of this book, your relationship will be strengthened through your practice.

Bless you!

Important Etiquette Points for your partner's full knowledge:

1. *Respect should be shown to the elderly, your parents, your in-laws – if you are married – to teachers, your boss, authority, and those who have earned a place in the community for their work and good behavior.*
2. *Respect the individuality of your partner.*
3. *Remember and celebrate important dates.*
4. *Do not limit your spouse's goals and dreams.*
5. *Do not betray his/her trust.*
6. *Do not ridicule him/her.*
7. *Apply all the standards of good behavior, especially with our life partner.*

Conclusion

One day after a romantic night with my husband - on a trip to Mexico - we were chatting animatedly and suddenly he said to me, "Why do you not write a book about sexual protocol?" You can imagine my laughter; and, above all, my friends who have known me all their lives know that, the subject is not one that I would discuss with any of them, nor with my family. Only with my husband. I studied from the ages of three to eighteen in Catholic schools. Where they recommended that if you had a bad thought, you prayed that it would disappear. As these bad thoughts grew, they hinted that those desires that, with the changes of adolescence, might arrive to a girl. One day, I confessed when I was fourteen years old, because I was so excited to see the romantic film – "Maria"– based on the book by the Colombian writer, Jorge Isaac.

For us, talking about sex was considered something very personal. Therefore, it was not the kind of topic that I talked with my mother or my sisters, and currently, I do not do it with my daughters either. It did not used to be the topic of an afternoon of women's reunion. I think the most pornographic thing I heard from a relative was from a great-aunt who married a man in his forties at the age – when I was only excited about a romantic film – fourteen years old. Her husband by the way, died fourteen years later, leaving her, a noticeably young widower. One day and in a low voice - like who is going to tell you a confidence - she told me the following: "Your great uncle and I made love in the dark, and then we had to go to the river to bathe." They were landowners and I did not want to ask questions about it. For example, like: Why did they not bathe in the shower? I would have died of grief before asking such a question. However, I was curious and perhaps if that comment had been made to me in this century, perhaps I would have been more liberal in asking certain kinds of questions about some details of what happened between my great-uncle and her.

Today half a century later, on my return to Florida - where I reside - I decided that instead of writing about sexual protocol, I was going to research and write about the protocol and etiquette that a person has to have towards a partner to grow up successfully. Unfortunately, there is not much information related to this type of protocol. However, I accepted the challenge that this, my sixth book, which could be considered the seventh if we take the second edition of Living in Harmony as another book – could gather some ideas for you. Those young people – and those not so young – who want to find the ideal partner. Especially for millennial couples who yearn for success and know what the protocol and the etiquette are to keep their partner until death separates them.

I must stress that if with our siblings – who come from the same father, same mother or both parents – we are not alike even though our genes and environment were the same, we cannot expect our partner to have the same perspectives of the life that we do. There will be points of view that will coincide and others where they will have to negotiate harmoniously. Since this is precisely the interesting thing about coexistence, it is important to consider that our partner is not our copy, since, if so, it would be very boring. The fun is in growing up and even getting old together. Always trying to remember that love does not disappear and that it continually transforms through our behavior, and the needs that arise during our coexistence; and as we get older. Of course, there will also be situations and gestures that, with coexistence, will help us to seem more and more alike every day.

We know we do not have the absolute truth. Before we demand our partner to be perfect, we must reflect on how we act. It is advisable for our sake, and that of the people around us, to try to be better human beings in our day to day; therefore, it is not advisable to use the word divorce or separation as an outlet for any problem or momentary circumstance. Every night before bed, examine your day and think you can do better at the next sunrise. Analyzing our actions daily will be used in various situations, such as circumstances that warrant especially important decisions, whether in the field of work or family. We will also use it in less relevant situations of our existence, as in a social event. For example: an office meeting or home party with family, friends, and children – if they have them. Think carefully about every detail: the music, the amount of food and drink, who will be the guests, the decoration, etc. If after the event everything was a success... congratulations! If you can – together – improve any detail, take note of it! even if you keep this information in your minds to improve the details needed next time.

Remember that every act you perform in your home must possess the best energy possible. Do not stop updating in your professional careers, and in your personal life both in the current topics, and in terms of better coexistence. As you well know we study several years to practice a profession. On the other hand, for an issue as important as our family – often – we do not give it the importance that it truly deserves. Sometimes we handle situations as best we can; and as we are better able to be, the chances of being successful in the goals we set ourselves will always be greater. Considering that what we start, we must finish it very well and not half-heartedly, until it is completed in its entirety.

We want reputable brands in everything related to our exterior – clothing, perfume or cologne, shoes and other accessories - that give us the appearance of being exemplary and successful people, but we should be consistent and give it the same importance to be exemplary people demonstrating good writing, having conversations where we manifest an excellent general culture – remember that words are stronger than looks – we should know how to behave appropriately in various situations and also, the most important point, have we managed to have control over ourselves?

It is important to always give a personal touch to everything we do, to the relationship with our partner. Like, for example, bringing breakfast to bed on Sundays to that special being, taking care of every detail. Such as placing it on the tray: the right dish accompanied by its cutlery, glass, cup, salt and napkin on the right side – the left – and as a small detail we will put a flower in a small vase. In addition, we will sweetly liven up this special moment that we have prepared for our beloved, with a romantic background music. With details like that, how can he or she not love you?

As we reach the conclusion of this book, it means that you have already covered the seven (7) chapters, where I hope you have enjoyed them one by one, page by page; and notice, that the information contained is based on the traditional point of view, combined with the current era. To give you tools that are favorable to you in your relationship. These tools are the product of knowledge from the information collected, academic studies, real examples and experience gathered over the years of my existence so that, with these ideas and your own conclusions, you can achieve a love relationship which has a happy and successful ending.

It will be a pleasure for me to know your opinions, suggestions, comments and even those constructive criticisms that may contribute something good for the following editions.

Long live sex! If it makes sense, but above all...
Long live The Protocol and Etiquette for Successful

Couples! It helps us to have ideas, rules, and norms to treasure better human relationships.

About the author

Yelina Nieto

Yelina Nieto was born in Venezuela where she completed her primary and secondary studies at a prestigious school for ladies in Caracas, her hometown. She graduated with a Bachelor of Science degree in civil engineering in Worcester, Massachusetts. She has lived in three Latin American countries, in several cities in the United States and spends long periods in Germany. Her favorite pastime is to travel, getting to know other cultures and enjoying the gastronomy of different places in the world. She is sociable and always finds reasons to have a party, meeting or food at home and thus enjoy the company of family and friends. Married to her great companion and inspiration of many of her books, Oliver Neumeister, together they have five children: two from Oliver's first marriage and three from Yelina's first marriage. And they have an excellent relationship between all of them. In addition, Yelina and Oliver are already grandparents to several beautiful grandchildren.

She has had the pleasure of meeting educated people from different cultures and from various countries. She always comments that good manners are not only useful for the aristocracy in Europe or other parts of the world, but for everyone. In addition to her bachelor’s degree as a Civil Engineer, Yelina Nieto, has attended various courses among which we can mention neuroscience, creative writing, sales courses, Feng Shui practices, Reiki, conferences on Zen Coaching, and several related to human psychology, emphasizing women. In addition, she has completed diploma programs in finance, in the history of religions; and, on protocol and etiquette, a topic to which she has given more emphasis in recent years. Her ideal is that the knowledge she has acquired through her studies, travel, and life experiences, will be useful to others. This desire is her motivation to sit for many hours to write, and thus embody in her books the same desire in the reader to show empathy and encourage good behavior into practice. Then the world will be much better for all.

Literary works by the author:

El Protocolo y la Etiqueta: de una Pareja Exitosa, Yelina A Nieto| February, 2020

La Convivencia en Armonía: Practicando la "Buena Educación", en nuestro día a día (2da. edición). Yelina A Nieto | July, 2019

Mas de 100 Ciudades Visitadas y más de 10 Vividas: Mi experiencia resumida de vivir 40 años fuera de Venezuela. Yelina A Nieto | June, 2018

El A B C: de la Buena Educación. Yelina A Nieto | March, 2018

Sofie y los Buenos Modales. Yelina A Nieto| April, 2017

Hagamos de una casa, un Hogar. Yelina A Nieto/ Ofelia Hernández | April, 2011

La Convivencia en Armonía: Practicando la "Buena Educación", en nuestro día a día (1ra. edición). Yelina A Nieto | May, 2008.

REFERENCES

Alegría, C., (2018). ***Sexo Sagrado,*** CreativeSpace, Columbia, S.C.

Antillón, F., M., (1979). ***Cortesía y urbanidad en la vida diaria,*** Lehmann Editores, Costa Rica.

Baldrige L., (1985). ***Complete guide to executive manners***, Rawson Associates, Pennsylvania.

Bethanne, P., (2011). ***An Uncommon History of Common Courtesy***, Washington, D.C.

Carreño, M., A., (1853). ***El Manual de Urbanidad y Buenas Maneras,*** Caracas.

Dumas, P. & Lesur, L., (2005). ***Le convive comme il faut,*** Aubin Imprimeur, Francia.

Eichler, L., (1958). ***Nuevo Libro de Etiqueta***, Ediciones Hymsa, Barcelona.

Gillmann, D., (2015). ***Knigge für Dummies,*** Munich.

Gordoa, V., (2007). ***El Poder de la Imagen Pública,*** México.

Hamel, M., (1984). ***Sex Etiquette,*** New York.

Johnson D., (2010). ***The Little Book of Etiquette,*** Philadelphia.

Labón, C., R., (2006). ***En Jeans, pero con Modales***, Trillas, México.

Losada, C., (2006). ***Protocolo moderno y éxito social***, Alianza Editorial, Madrid.

Neumeister, T., (2018). ***Tatiana's ABC of Good Manners,*** Múnich.

Perrier-Robert, A., (2011). ***Ideas para Servir la mesa***, Madrid.

Post P., (2004). ***Etiquette***, New York.

Schillebeeckx, E., (1970). ***El Matrimonio, realidad terrena y misterio de salvación,*** Ediciones Sígueme, Salamanca.

Schmidt-Decker, P., (1995) ***Das grosse Buch des guten Benehmens***, ECON Verlag, Alemania.

Selecciones del Reader's Digest, (2006). ***¿Somos amables?*** *Prueba internacional de cortesía,* México.

Spade, K., (2004). ***Manners***, Italia.

Vargas, G., (2000). ***El arte de convivir y la cortesía social.*** Editorial Planeta, México.

Vilar, E., (1973). ***El Varón Domado***. Grijalbo, Barcelona.

Zúñiga, A., (2006). ***Etiqueta Moderna***, Colombia.

Zingg, M., & Aranaga, M., (2010). ***Glamour para llevar***, Caracas.

REFERENCES FROM THE INTERNET

@alfonso feliz (2015). https://www.encontrarse.com/n/51523-por-que-la-gente-grita-cuento-tibetano.

Bernal, Paola, (2013). Reglas de Etiqueta en Pareja, Vanguardia, Colombia.

Emol, (2011). Protocolo Sexual, Emol, Chile.

E P Mundo, (2018*)*. Quiénes son los que mejor besan de acuerdo con el zodiaco.

Debayle, Martha, (2017). El secreto de las parejas que perduran, México.

Hernández, L., Protocolo de pareja en espacios públicos para que su relación funcione, Berelleza.

@Integrandoelser, (2019). Los 5 lenguajes del Amor, Integrando el ser, Madrid.

https://lifeobsessions.wordpress.com/2012/06/19/liking-vs-loving-pleito-de-amar-y-querer-a-poem-by-andres-eloy-blanco-8-2/

www.ingramcontent.com/pod-product-compliance
Lightning Source LLC
Chambersburg PA
CBHW040129270326
41928CB00001B/5
9781733648974